WHAT I HAVE

is

ENOUGH

WHAT I HAVE *is* ENOUGH

Tuning Your Life
to *your*
God-Given
Potential

Leslie Fatai

CFI
An imprint of Cedar Fort, Inc.
Springville, Utah

ISBN 13: 978-1-4621-2245-5

Published by CFI, an imprint of Cedar Fort, Inc.
2373 W. 700 S., Springville, UT 84663
Distributed by Cedar Fort, Inc., www.cedarfort.com

Library of Congress Cataloging-in-Publication Data on file.

Cover design by Wes Wheeler
Cover design © 2018 Cedar Fort, Inc.
Edited by Justin Greer and Lisa Christensen Hahne
Typeset by Kaitlin Barwick

Printed in the United States of America

10 9 8 7 6 5 4 3 2 1

Printed on acid-free paper

I dedicate this book to you who may be second-guessing yourself. You CAN do it!

And to my wonderful husband, Ofa, and our four beautiful children: Isa, Lepi, Gumi, and Dempsey. Thanks for leaving me alone to write this. I love you!

CONTENTS

CHAPTER 1

My Staff. My Score.

Music. My window to heaven. It was the language God first spoke to me. It's been one of my greatest teachers in helping me understand the world around me. Music would take me on a journey and sometimes even bring my pain and suffering to the forefront, but after experiencing the power of music, it would heal me every time. I tried to hide, but music would find me—the real me. It challenged me many times reminding me of my true self, moving me to experience places I never imagined I'd see or feel, and it allows me to revel in my insecurities and discover the glorious beauty behind it all. And as I am trying to figure out this thing called life, music has connected me to the deepest parts of my soul and I cannot deny its truth: I am whole.

When I first started learning about music, the properties and different elements of it just made sense to me. The melody, harmony, rhythm, tone, dynamics, texture, and the form—I understood how everything had a purpose and its own specific work to make music. The best part about it? Music could be anything its creator wanted it to be. In order for me to freely create the music I wanted to create, I had to understand the rules and the direction I wanted to take. I had to understand how it could serve its purpose in *my* song and what boundaries

I wanted to create, explore, and even push. And so with every blank piece of paper or blank staff of sheet music, I would always ask a series of questions: Who are you? What do you want to say? Where are we going to take this? It was as if these songs had a life of their own calling me to tell a story, and most of the time it was my own.

I was born a rainbow baby. A rainbow baby is a baby who's born after a miscarriage. My mom always reminded me of the miscarriage she had the year before I was born. I don't think it had a big effect on me except that she frequently told me I was special. I would think it was because I was born with only five fingers, but my mom would always say I was meant to come to them as their firstborn child.

I was born to two Tongan immigrants who migrated to the United States in the early '80s. My parents, who spoke little English, were thrown into a whole new world when I entered their lives. I instantly became a member of the disabled community with an unknown future ahead of me—so they thought. Now being a parent myself, I can only imagine how it must have been for them, but I know one thing that my parents had that helped them through it all: faith. If there's one thing I do not doubt, it's their faith in God and His divine plan for each of us.

Both my parents are converts to The Church of Jesus Christ of Latter-day Saints. My mom was born and raised in the Methodist faith and was baptized into the Church of Jesus Christ at age eleven, along with her family. She and several of her siblings served missions for the Church. Shortly after serving a mission in Tonga, she migrated to the United States. My dad grew up in the Catholic faith. He comes from a strong devout Catholic family, and three of his seventeen siblings (and several of his nieces and nephews) have entered the Catholic clergy and ministry. Each of his siblings and their families are faithful, strong members of their faith. Only two of his siblings are Latter-day Saints.

My father's conversion story is one of my favorites. He unknowingly gained a testimony of the Book of Mormon when he was fourteen years old when he saw his village's collection of burnt trash under a lychee tree. Beside the pile, he saw a ripe lychee fruit on the ground. It looked like it had just fallen from the tree. He was hungry and decided to get the fruit. As he picked up the fruit, he noticed a burnt book under it. Curious, he opened it and was surprised to see the pages inside undamaged. Reading one page in the book convinced him it was true. He remembers reading only ten verses, and it was all about Jesus Christ, with the word *Nifai* (the Tongan spelling of the name Nephi) on the top of the page. It would take three years for him to learn the title of that burnt book when he started meeting with Latter-day Saint missionaries and learned more of the Book of Mormon and of the restored gospel. He soon desired to be baptized.

The day my father was baptized, my grandfather had severely beaten him and had declared him disowned from the family for betraying the family's faith, traditions, and values. He was thrown out of the home with his belongings. At the time, my grandfather was serving as the *tauhi* for their congregation, which is similar to being the bishop in an LDS congregation. As a recent convert with nowhere to go, he was taken in by my husband's family. My father and my husband's father come from the same village of Matahau, Tongatapu, Tonga. One of my father's fondest memories while staying there was being greeted every morning to hymns being beautifully sung and being taught the restored gospel every day. They supported and nourished his faith and testimony through their acts of love and service during a difficult time in his life.

Soon thereafter, he decided to serve a mission for the Church. The mission deepened his conversion to Jesus Christ, and many lives were blessed for his faithful service as a missionary, including my own. After he served his mission, he strongly desired to be married and sealed in the temple. At the time, there were no temples in Tonga. The closest temple was the Hamilton New Zealand Temple, but despite the distance, my father decided to marry in the Salt Lake City Temple. He did all he could to prepare for the trip to the United States to be married in the Salt Lake City Temple. When he left Tonga, he was engaged to be married to someone other than my mother. When he got to the States, his plans fell through with her, and it would take a couple years before he found my mom. When they finally met, they only dated for a month and were soon married in the Salt Lake City Temple with only $300 in his pocket to start their family.

A little over a year after they wed, I was born. In Tonga, the culture is matriarchal. Usually the oldest female child is known as the *fahu* and is honored in behalf of her brother's children. The *fahu* acts as the family matriarch and is given honors as well as responsibilities for formal and informal family occasions. In this particular situation of my birth, my father, as per Tongan tradition, sought from my *fahu*, his sister, a name for his first-born child. His sisters living in the United States fulfilled this role for my *fahu*, and they decided on a name for me. They unanimously decided on the name of their mother, my grandmother, Lesieli Fatai. My mom wanted my first name to be an English name and chose Leslie since it was close to Lesieli; but as I was growing up, I was always called by my middle name, Fatai. This was the name we called Grandma.

I have always felt deeply connected with my grandmother. There's a scripture in the Book of Mormon that I hold dear to my heart because of her. The prophet Helaman had two sons, Nephi and Lehi. I love what he told his sons regarding their names. He said, "Behold, I have given unto you the names of our first parents who came out of the land of Jerusalem; and this I have done that when you remember your names ye may remember them; and when ye remember them ye may remember their works; and when ye remember their works ye may know how that it is said . . . that they were good" (Helaman 5:6). Let me tell you about my grandmother.

Born in 1921 in 'Ahau, Tongatapu, Tonga, Lesieli Fatai was the oldest of seven children. She met my grandfather and married him at the age of eighteen. They had fourteen children together. My father is number eleven, and I am grandchild number forty-seven for her. The first time I met Grandma Fatai was at a family reunion in Minneapolis, Minnesota, in 1994 when I was eight years old. The only thing I remember from that first meeting was realizing that she was in fact a real person. Up until that point, I had only been told stories of her.

It wasn't until 1996 that I started getting to know my grandmother. We flew out to Tonga for another family reunion. In every family reunion we always start and end with a family prayer and a Catholic mass service led by one of my uncles or cousins. It was in these services and family prayers that I would hear Grandma sing. She had a powerful soprano voice. I remember thinking, *That lady can sing high!* Those high notes she sang would pierce right through you. I've been told stories of Grandma Fatai and how people from afar could hear her voice whenever she would sing in church or when she was working in the bush. Sometimes she could be heard all the way from the next village. She was known as an entertainer and loved to dance and sing. She was a songwriter and also a choreographer and arranged and taught many original songs and choreography of different Tongan traditional dances.

Besides her many talents, the one thing that is always mentioned about her is her work ethic. Anyone who ever knew my grandmother would have some story about how hard she worked to provide for her family. And not just for her husband and children, but for her younger siblings and their families as well. Although I met her late in her life, I was able to see and walk through the plantation fields she worked in from morning to night. I visited the farmers market where she would spend hours selling her crops. I got to see and walk on the school grounds where my father and his siblings attended, and learned how she would pay their school fees with her crops when money was scarce. I'll never forget walking inside the humble hut she raised her children in using only a clothesline and a bed sheet to divide the one room into two. The kitchen was outside of the hut and I saw where she would cook in the earth oven, also known in the Pacific Islands as the *umu*, a traditional cooking style of the islands where food was cooked underground in a hole. I learned of how she made sure there was food for everyone to eat.

Grandma was a lot of things. She was strong in every way, faithful, loyal, hardworking, humorous, and sassy. So many stories would leave me laughing at Grandma's sassiness and how she didn't take crap from no one. I also saw a glimpse into her heart when my dad shared how even after he was disowned from his family for joining the Church, Grandma Fatai, unbeknownst to her husband, would still come looking for him to make sure he was okay. I have always felt empowered from my name because of her. My mom told me that was one of the reasons why they wanted to name me after her—she was a strong woman. And not knowing what the future looked like for me, my mom was encouraged with the name given to me.

I still think about Grandma Fatai and imagine how she would handle my struggles today. I only met her three times before she passed away, but to this day people still share stories with me about her strength, her work ethic, and her many talents. The memories shared have deepened my appreciation not only for her but also for all my ancestors who came before me. The legacies our forefathers left behind, the sacrifices they made, the struggles they endured, and the trials that tested their faith empower me. If they triumphed, I can too.

I was fortunate to have five younger siblings. My parents planned on having us kids close in age. They had six kids in seven years, and each of them is so different. My two brothers born after me are complete opposites: Edward is my serious and responsible brother, while Dempsey is my goofy, witty, and free-spirited brother. My mom admitted that she was hoping for a girl each pregnancy after my birth, and she finally got what she wished for with the birth of my sister Vicelia. Vicelia was everything my mom hoped for. She got lucky again and gave birth to my baby sister, Keturah. We expected the youngest of the bunch to be another girl, and my mom felt relieved it was going to be a girl, but we were all surprised when my baby brother, Ekuasi, came instead. None of my siblings were born with any deformities or disabilities, and neither did my parents have any disabilities or have any history of it in their families. I was meant to be the one.

I know each of my siblings was meant to come when they came because each of them continue to influence my life in some way to this day. Through the good and especially through the bad, I have learned how much I really need them and how much they need me. I know they would have something to say about that, but the honest truth is we all need each other. Whether it's the family you were born into or given to, or maybe the people we choose to surround ourselves with, they all affect us positively and negatively. It's important to understand the necessity of both. The real power is in your choice to react, especially when it comes to things you cannot change.

I was born with a limb deficiency with my arms. From my elbows down to my fingertips, they are deformed. Doctors told my mother that they stopped developing in the womb. My left arm is my dominant arm, and I do the majority of everything with it. I can bend and move my arm easily. I also have more fingers on my left hand than my right. My right arm is my support arm. It is stick thin and won't ever get bigger because I'm unable to bend my elbow and work out those muscles. It often aches from not being able to bend, but I'm able to flex it to ease the aches. My two fingers on my right arm have very little movement. I have to physically move the little finger (They are both little, but there's a littler finger) in order for it to do what I want it to do. For example, when I play the piano I usually drag that finger on the keys to where I need it to go and then push.

Because of the limitations of my right hand, I can't hold anything heavier than three pounds without the support of my other hand or my body. I struggled to fix my hair, button my shirt, put jewelry on, or even put deodorant on. I never understood how much my mom did for me until she started working. One morning, my mom had to work early, so my dad was left with the task of fixing my hair. I was ten at the time, and girls my age could at least put their hair in a ponytail. I couldn't. My dad put my hair in a ponytail and it was crooked, bumpy, and just ugly. I cried. But because I really wanted my hair in a ponytail that day, I kept it. It wasn't until Vicelia and Keturah got a little older that they started helping me.

Like Edward and Dempsey, my sisters, Vicelia and Keturah, are also complete opposites. Vicelia is my loud, outspoken, energetic, and sassy sister. She is a busy bee, smiling, talking, singing, and dancing. She was the one who spent the most time in the kitchen cooking with Mom—hence the reason why she's the best cook out of us all. She's very intelligent and creative and is naturally gifted in the performing arts. Keturah is my quiet, soft-spoken, thoughtful, and genuinely kind sister. She loves animals, is athletic, and is very intelligent. She was called the serious baby because she rarely smiled. She was the only sister who could hang with my brothers when they played sports, and we sometimes joked that she should've been a boy. Despite being quiet, she is very conscientious in all she does and will speak up when she feels it is necessary to do so.

When I started junior high school, I needed help getting ready in the mornings for school. Vicelia and Keturah were in second and third grade at the time. Most mornings, I turned to Vicelia to help me since she was older, but they both helped me nonetheless. The biggest thing they helped me with was fixing my hair. As a teenager in middle school, I wanted my hair to be perfect, especially since I started liking boys.

One morning, Vicelia must've put my hair in a ponytail at least ten times. There would always be one thing I didn't like as I would point out it was crooked or it was too high or just wasn't good enough, and she would take the rubber band out and start all over again. At the time, I didn't know if I was more frustrated with her or with myself. Some mornings would be a struggle as my sisters would begrudgingly fix my hair with tears streaming down their tired faces as they would appease my early-morning demands.

Feeling their frustration frustrated me. The same dialogue, more or less, would run through my mind over and over again: *Here we go again! She doesn't want to do my hair. I know it. Wait! Did she just mumble something? Sheesh! I don't even want to ask you for your help, but my freakin' arm can't freakin' bend and I can't hold my hair up. Ugh! I wish I had magic powers so I don't have to ask you. Dang! That would be so tight if I did!* I would imagine how perfect my hair would be if my hands were normal and I could fix it myself. The amazing thing about it all is that my sisters helped me even when they didn't want to, and although this frustration has been an emotional roller coaster for me, it has been more so for them.

My brothers, on the other hand, didn't fix my hair often (though there were times that they did). They were my last resort. The relationship I have with my brothers is different. My parents had Edward, Dempsey, and me back to back. Because we were so close in age, almost all of my favorite childhood memories included them. And if there's anything my brothers did, it was to give me the normalcy my parents wanted.

My mom was the kind of mother who would have us all in matching outfits and coordinated our outfits with theirs. Edward and Dempsey were often times mistaken as twins growing up, especially in their matching outfits and mushroom haircuts. And how could I forget the mountainous curly bangs with the itchy puff-sleeved dresses my mom would dress me in?

Because Edward is the oldest boy, my parents expected a lot from him growing up, and it was quite evident in the way he carried himself. He has a quiet dignity about himself. He doesn't like to be in the spotlight and is a natural-born leader. I always had a hard time arguing with him because he usually spoke the truth and made sure he said the last word. But out of all my siblings, he is the most competitive.

Once we had a sword fight and decided to up the ante by using real knives. We got the longest and biggest knives we could find in the kitchen. As we engaged in our battle, I lunged forward to attack and Edward deflected my move catching my right forearm with his blade. I didn't feel a thing at first as I stared at his knife in my arm, but when the blood started to trickle, it finally clicked in my brain that I was in pain. Hearing me screaming at the top of my lungs, Mom rushed in and bandaged my wound—all while yelling at the both of us for being stupid playing with the knives. We learned our lesson then, and I've never played with real knives again.

My relationship with Dempsey is a special one because he is one of a kind. You know how there's that one sibling who just knows which buttons to push to get you mad and does it just for fun? That was Dempsey. As we got older, his jokes and witty comebacks would have us mad, crying, laughing, or all of the above. He had a way of using humor to diffuse his anger because I rarely saw him mad. But when he was mad, he was *mad*. It was like he was the Incredible Hulk. You just had to move and get out of the way or he'd throw a mean punch in your face.

Dempsey didn't care what others thought about him. In high school, I'll never forget the first time he went to school wearing Vicelia's size-nine pink flip flops on his size-thirteen Tongan feet. These flip flops had a big flower on top that was bedazzled with a fake diamond stud, I kid you not, and all heads turned towards those pink flip flops as he walked down the main hallway. I noticed some people just whispering to their neighbor and pointing to his flip flops while others were giggling, but I'll never forget his friends walking beside him like he was so cool.

I never understood some of his fashion choices growing up, but I always admired his confidence and others embraced him for it in all his uniqueness. He, also, is a natural-born leader and an optimist to a fault. If he wanted to do something, he'd do it.

But this got him into a lot of trouble growing up and made for some unforgettable memories.

In elementary school, my parents made the rule to come straight home after school. When Dempsey started first grade, he made lots of friends. Edward and I would head home after school, but Dempsey would head to a friend's house and return home late. One day, my dad got fed up with it and had a little suitcase waiting for him. When Dempsey came home, Dad told him to pack his clothes and all his belongings. He was moving out and moving in with his friend's family—*his* new family.

Dempsey stood there in disbelief. Edward and I stood there in disbelief. My dad said it for probably the fifth time before Dempsey finally went to his room and started to pack. Edward and I cried as we watched him gather his stuff. I turned to Edward and asked, "Let's say a prayer?" He agreed as we went to our parents' room to say our prayer. As annoying as Dempsey was as a little brother, we didn't want him to leave our family. He was our brother. We did actually love him. After we said our prayer, we went looking for Dempsey.

My dad was at the front door waiting, and there was Dempsey with his belongings walking slowly toward the door. Edward and I started crying again. My dad looked at us and then at Dempsey and asked, "Do you want to live with your friend and his family?"

Dempsey cried, "No! I want to live here!" He asked us if we wanted him to leave. We cried no. Although my dad tried to hide it, I saw him smile but only for a moment. He wanted to prove how serious he was about us coming home after school. It was safe to say my dad was never planning on giving Dempsey away, but he scared us all that night.

With the age gap between me and the three youngest siblings, I didn't get to know them until they were teenagers.

I've always thought they were very talented compared to my brothers and me. We started having a fun rivalry between the older three and the younger three siblings. My brothers and I went to Granger High School. The younger siblings went to Hunter High School. These two schools are about three and a half miles apart and are well-known rivals in our hometown of West Valley City.

As my younger siblings started going to Hunter, my brothers and I would always talk trash and throw shade at them for betraying the family's allegiance to Granger. Because Hunter's color is blue and Granger's color is red, my brothers would sport some kind of red or Granger gear at their Hunter games, especially when they were playing against each other. At first, we refused to say, "Go, Hunter!" but as we got older, we realized how childish we were and focused more on being there to support each other. So, there we were cheering for our siblings and cheering for Hunter.

That was something my father instilled in us, and he made sure that we did everything together. If someone had a game or a performance, everyone had to go support. I was the only sibling not involved in any sports, so I was designated as the cameraman and cheerleader. I did have my music, and my family did the same in supporting me whenever I performed.

Coming to America has afforded my parents opportunities they would not have had back on the islands. They have remained close to their immediate and extended families, and I've seen them help our extended family in different ways—and I have seen that help reciprocated back to us. My parents have an open-door policy, and when I was growing up, if anyone needed a place to stay, our home was always open. My dad would make sure the needs of whoever stayed in our home were met temporally and spiritually.

It was also fun to live nearby aunties and uncles. When the weather was warm, we cousins would always get together to play. Our families were close and spent a lot of time with each other. Many summer days would be spent at the park eating lunch and playing for hours until it was time to go home for dinner. Mom would be sitting with my aunties crocheting another blanket and talking story. When we were lucky, my cousins and I would get wet playing with the park's sprinklers, spraying each other down to see who got sprayed the most. We definitely had some great memories (and some we wish we could forget).

What's a childhood without getting yourself into some mischief and causing some—or a lot of—trouble? Well, one summer we caused a lot of trouble. I was five years old, and my two younger brothers were ages four and three. My parents were getting their food storage and emergency kits ready. They had many barrels, boxes, and buckets filled with all kinds of things we would need in any case of an emergency. They had a room set aside in our basement filled with some of those boxes and buckets, and everything else was stored outside either in the backyard or in the trailer parked on the driveway.

My brothers and I loved to be outside exploring the yard playing pretend. We found in the trailer a bucket filled with matchbooks. We started lighting them and instantly became fascinated with each flame. We quickly got bored lighting one match and started lighting the whole matchbook. Eager to keep the fire going, we started looking for things we could burn. We burned leaves, sticks, paper, plastic, bugs, food, and even our mini trampoline. Mom was furious when she discovered what we did and banished us from playing with matches again.

I wish I could say that we listened, but we didn't. When our cousins came over, we stole a matchbook from the bucket my dad hid to show them our newest discovery. They instantly became hooked, and we all loved our new game. We started burning little piles of junk lying around the yard and would try to keep the fire burning. It was always fascinating as we all huddled around the little fire, *ooh*-ing and *aah*-ing, watching the stuff burn away. We planned to meet the next day at our aunty's house to burn more things.

While mom was sleeping, we climbed out the basement window, took some more matchbooks, and crossed over to our aunty's house. She lived the next street over, and we were lucky that we knew a shortcut to her house. My uncle lived across the street from us, so we crossed through his yard, which was connected to Aunty's backyard. We loved going to Aunty's house because she had a big trampoline and a garage filled with fun toys, including a boat we'd all play pretend in as if we were out at sea. As we got to the house, our cousins were waiting for us with several piles of trash ready to burn. We were all excited to be together and play our new game again. Some of us started burning stuff out on the driveway while the rest of us were in the garage.

Dempsey and our oldest cousin, Junior, were getting bored and decided to get in the boat. They climbed in and said, "Let's make a fire!" As they started their fire, the seats quickly caught on fire. As they watched the fire grow, Junior was able to jump out of the boat. Dempsey was only three years old and was too small to jump out like Junior had. Dempsey was crying, and I remember thinking, *How do we get Dempsey out?*

As I watched him crying for help and trying his best to avoid the growing flames, one of our cousins ran inside the house to get help. Lucky for us, Uncle Mailoni was downstairs. As he came out, we all yelled, "Get Dempsey! He's inside the boat! We need to get him out!" He quickly ran to the boat, threw a blanket over Dempsey, grabbed him, and pulled him out to safety. He ushered all of us kids away from the garage and moved us next door to the neighbor's front yard. By that time the garage had caught on fire and the fire was starting to move toward the house. We were soon placed in bins filled with water. We all congratulated Dempsey for not dying and continued to play as if nothing had happened.

We would frequently comment on the growth of the black smoke in the sky. Soon we heard sirens grow louder and louder. The fire truck had arrived, and the firefighters came to put the fire out. We were excited they had come. We continued to have fun in the water. One by one, our parents came and took us home. Mom arrived, panting and trying to catch her breath. She was pregnant with Keturah at the time. She looked like she just woke up and from a bad dream. She had a terrified look on her face. I knew we were in trouble: one, for sneaking out of the house, and two, for stealing the matches. She motioned us to come to her, and we headed back home.

The sirens had woken mom up. She looked outside and saw Aunty's house on fire and instantly knew we were there. She immediately ran down the street toward Aunty's house. The police had already arrived and had blocked off the street and were keeping anyone from entering. She exclaimed, "My kids are at that house!" They let her through and as she got closer, she saw us playing with our cousins. Surprisingly, my mom was not angry with us when we got home. She was more so relieved and concerned for us. She hugged each of us tightly and I'll never forget that. Despite the reckless things I did as a child, my parents always loved me. I have never doubted my parents' love for me, but there were times when I did question how they showed it. I've come to know my parents did their very best for me and my siblings in our upbringing.

Something my mom admitted to not liking about my adolescence were the constant stares I received. "People were so curious and they would watch you. I didn't like it," she'd say as she shared the difference between when someone was looking in curiosity and when someone was looking down on me. Her protective instinct would kick in, and she would glare at them as she would take me away. For me, now as a mother myself, I can't help but imagine the questions that she had and if she ever felt guilty for having me, a child with a disability. Was it something she ate during her pregnancy? Did she do something wrong in those nine months that caused my limbs from forming completely? Was this God punishing her? Despite these natural feelings of guilt, shame, and worry, I'm grateful my mom saw a bigger picture and had faith in God's plan for the both of us. She strongly believed there was a reason why I came to them the way I came when I came.

When I was growing up, she strived to instill in me an overbearing confidence in myself. I say "overbearing" because my mother wanted to make sure that I was never taken advantage of and that if someone made fun of me I could handle myself. She unknowingly fostered a bossy diva. I say I was bossy because I really felt like the boss growing up—it came with the territory of being the oldest. Ask my siblings about it and you'll never hear the end of it.

I have to say I'm grateful my parents didn't treat me any different from my siblings. I had chores just like them. I went to the same schools as them. I had to dance in our family's Polynesian show even though my hands were moving very different than everyone else's. They didn't want me to feel different or left out (although I would've loved to have been left out when we all got in trouble and got punished). They never labeled me or said I couldn't do this or that. They just let me be to have fun as a child exploring the world around me. Honestly, they didn't know what to expect from me and waited to see what I was going to do in my life. They did their best to teach and raise me into the person God knew I was to be.

CHAPTER 2

Song Selection

I feel like life itself is a song. We each have a song that is unique to us. The challenge is learning to perform *your* song and performing it well. The advantage? You choose an instrument that can best showcase your song and you choose how you want to play it. That instrument is like your talents, your skills, your interests, and your passions in life. How you use your instrument affects your song.

I've had to struggle to hear my life's song. Most times I could hear it clearly, but other times I've had to dig deep inside and find it. My hands are a crucial part of my song—I've struggled to learn that. My hands have taught me to see things differently in life, and I have cultivated a vision that goes beyond my two physical eyes. It is a vision of potential, of second chances, of exploration, and of acceptance.

I learned early on that I was never meant to fit in. I tried, but because I did things differently, I stood out. I'm not going to lie, I'm still not used to standing out and the having the attention that being different brings me. I've always had to think outside of the box, but I've learned that this is an advantage for me because it takes me longer to give up. I've asked myself many times whether I have exhausted all possibilities. "What if I try" are four words that have pushed me to explore my capabilities until I feel I can do no more.

For example, as a young child, I attempted to cross the monkey bars. I got a hold of the first bar. It was moving from that first bar to the next I could never get. My hands weren't strong enough to hold me up and I always fell. I even broke my two front teeth trying to cross the monkey bars. My new goal was to get to the second bar without falling. After many failed attempts, I decided it just wasn't my time yet. I still long to cross the monkey bars, and I don't know if I'll ever be able to, but I still try to cross it when my curiosity gets the best of me. I still fall each time, but I hope that one day I will get to that second bar.

I was surrounded with music all my life, thanks to my dad. He was my first mentor and teacher. He comes from a very talented family. His older sister, Vake, is the mother of the hit '80s group The Jets. She helped my father come to America in the early '80s. He spent time travelling with them as they toured around the states performing and would help out with their Polynesian show by playing and singing in the band. He did that with his sisters for a bit before settling down in Utah. I have only seen photos of them performing and heard stories of their performances and of life on the road.

In my youth, he shared with us his passion for performing. He had us learn Polynesian dances from different Pacific Islands and had us put on a Polynesian show for family gatherings. He taught us to sing and had us perform everywhere. But the one thing he didn't teach us was to play instruments, which is odd because he was a musician. One of my earliest memories of him is watching him and his band play. He played the guitar, piano, bass guitar, and even the drums. Many nights I would go to sleep listening to his band practice in our basement. They performed for all kinds of functions in churches, for weddings, family gatherings, and miscellaneous parties.

His band was another source of income, and it blessed our family in many ways. My dad would travel out of state and even out of the country to perform. There were only a few times I remember traveling as a family. I loved those trips because the other band members would bring their families and we'd play with the other kids. It was a lot of fun visiting new places and experiencing new things as a family. Out of all the things my dad expected us to do, he never expected us to play musical instruments. He simply said, "It's up to you if you want to learn to play or not," and that was that.

When I was in sixth grade, my music class had us learn to play an instrument that year. We were to take the instrument home and practice musical pieces as part of the music curriculum. I was excited to choose an instrument and curious to see which one I would end up choosing. As I looked at the string instruments, I knew I didn't have enough fingers to hold down the strings on a violin or the viola. The cello looked cool, but it was too big for me. Wind instruments were a negative. I decided to look at brass instruments and analyzed which one would suit me best. The trumpet looked promising. With only three finger buttons I would need to push, I felt it would be great to try it out. I quickly changed my mind though when I saw the trombone. All I had to do was slide the brace back and forth. I had enough fingers to do that, so I signed up for the trombone.

I was so excited the day we were able to take our instruments home. As soon as I got home, I went straight to my room to try it out. I put the trombone together, got my sheet music out, and started my first piece. I didn't make it past the first line before I came to the brutal realization that my arm was too short. *Why didn't I think of that?* I couldn't slide the brace far enough to reach the note I needed to play. This was frustrating but only for a moment. I quickly thought, *Hmm, how can I do this?*

So I tried switching the position of the trombone on my shoulder and hoped that it would make a difference. It didn't. It made it worse. I knew I had to keep it where I was taught to hold it. After I pondered for what seemed like hours, the thought came to mind to use my foot. I started to play the beginning of the piece using my hand. As the note approached for me to move the brace farthest from me, I switched from my hand to my foot. As I did that, the trombone fell. "Gosh!" I exclaimed, "Let's do that again."

Picking up the trombone, I started fiddling with the brace using my foot. *Wow!* I thought as I laughed out loud moving my foot forward and back towards my chest making sure my toes held its grip on the brace. *I look so funny,* I thought as I moved my foot. *I can't play like this in front of everyone. The other trombone players will be sitting up, and here am I with my foot up.* Mom came in to check on me midway through my foot performance. I was embarrassed and quickly shot my foot down. I didn't want to look at her, and so I continued to act as if I was busy figuring out my trombone. She left my room and I was alone to contemplate.

Feeling discouraged I decided I needed a break from practicing and went to get something to eat. Entering the kitchen, Mom greeted me with a few probing questions about the trombone. I sheepishly admitted to her, "I have to use my foot, Mom. It's the only way I can play it. I look so dumb." My mom listened intently trying to understand my dilemma and responded as any good parent does to don't give up. Honestly, that piece of advice went in one ear and out the other. I had already decided right then and there I wasn't going to play the trombone. It just wasn't for me. I mean, who plays the trombone with their foot? I do.

Funny thing is when I went back to my room, I had the urge to just try it again one more time. I hoped this time might be different like something would magically change as if the food I just ate had miraculously lengthened my arm in mere minutes. I was hopeful I would be able to play the song and reach every note, but I didn't. My arm still couldn't reach that far out. Flustered, I decided to use my foot again hoping maybe this time using my foot will be amazing and I'll be able to play the song. But no. It was even more embarrassing than the first time. I was literally laying on my back as I extended my foot out to reach that one stupid note. This wasn't going to work. I ended up returning the trombone back to my teacher and never looked back.

For some reason, my dad decided to tell everyone I was learning to play the trombone even after I returned it, and because he did that, I was invited to play for a marching band. Wouldn't that be a sight to see? The first foot trombone player in a marching band. Leaves you wondering how would I march in the band while my foot is playing. And although my attempt to play the trombone was short lived, that didn't stop me from exploring other instruments.

When we were younger, my dad's band room was off limits unless he was there. During some of his band practices, I would go in and sit and watch them and I would focus on their hands. I was mesmerized with their hand movements and how their fingers would dance with the strings. I would imagine how my hands would play their instrument and pretend I was playing along with them. As we got older, my dad allowed us to go in the band room on our own and play with the instruments.

I would go to each instrument and imitate each of my dad's band mates playing it with their facial expressions and body movements. My favorite instrument was the guitar. During my dad's performances, I would study him during his guitar solo and watch him be in the zone and get lost in the music. I never understood what he was doing until I found my instrument, the one instrument I could get lost in the music with.

We always had a keyboard. My dad used the keyboard frequently to teach us to sing or when we would perform as a family. We got a used piano years later when I was in high school. The piano wasn't my favorite instrument like the guitar, but it was the instrument I gravitated to the most. Those black and white keys became one of my greatest teachers. I can still remember vividly the first time those piano keys changed my life.

I was twelve years old and my family was at church for a ward activity. I was looking for my cousins and entered a room. There were kids in there playing the piano, so I decided to stay and listen. They soon left and I decided to sit there on the piano bench and play. The song I tried playing was "Mary Had a Little Lamb." As I started playing the melody of this very simple song, something amazing started to happen. I was in awe of what my hands were doing. I felt as if I had just woken up. Who would've thought this simple song could make me feel this way. It was exhilarating. I felt like I could do anything. And for the first time ever, I got a glimpse of my potential. I saw me. The real me. I was more than my body. I was more than my five fingers.

I was excited to go home and play on my dad's keyboard. As I got better playing "Mary Had a Little Lamb," I called my siblings to come hear me play. They listened just to be nice, but they didn't care. My brothers started playing "Mary Had A Little Lamb," and showed me up. I started thinking of other songs I could pick out on the keys, particularly songs using both hands. If I could do this, they would be impressed. I would sing songs and would play note-for-note each word I sang. I would feel excited again and learn a new song.

Because there was no YouTube back then to look up how to videos like there is today, we either had to find a teacher or learn from friends or family. At church, I would watch the other kids play the piano using both their hands. I would study their hand movements and commit to memory what I saw. I would then go to my keyboard and try to hit the same keys they pushed. It was hard trying to hit three notes with only two fingers, and I'll admit I was discouraged. I started listening to #1 songs on the radio at the time and would record them on a cassette tape, play it back, and learn it on the piano. The first song I learned was "All My Life," by K-Ci and JoJo. It took me a couple of months to learn the intro of that song. But with every new song I learned, it became easier to figure out. I was starting to see patterns.

Playing by ear was great, but at this time I was not satisfied. I wanted to learn more. I was envious of a girl who was always asked to play the piano at church. She played the piano beautifully and even knew how to play the organ. She was only a few years older than me and knew how to read music. I really wanted to learn how to read music only so I could get asked to play the piano on Sunday and play beautifully like her—or even better than her. Shame, I know, but she was that good and she inspired me to want to learn more. Yes, my intention at the time was not that great, but I am grateful for her today. Because of her talent, she inspired me to develop mine.

Sometimes we can feel less sure of ourselves and in our capabilities. Sometimes we may even question our worth. But I've learned some positives from comparison. We can make peace with our differences, we can inspire each other to be better, and even be happy for one another's triumphs. I could've focused on what I couldn't do which was play the piano like her and reading music, but after my "Mary Had A Little Lamb" epiphany, I knew deep down inside I could play like her if I was taught.

I asked my mom if I could take piano lessons, so she signed me up. My first lesson with my piano teacher was very interesting. I was excited to start playing like a real pianist, but was surprised to learn that the first lesson was about body and hand positioning. In the first couple pages of my piano book, there were pictures of how your body should be seated on the piano bench with your arms and hands properly placed on the keys to prevent any discomfort and pain. I distinctly remember her explaining the pictures in my book and asking me to mimic what I saw. I'll admit it was awkward at first, but I had to try.

She quietly sat there and waited to see what I was going to do. As I slowly placed my hands on the keys, I looked at my fingers thinking, *Which finger are you?* Even up to now, I have never decided which finger was a thumb, pinky, etc. It changes depending on what I need or how I feel at the time. So, I sat there and placed my fingers hoping, she wouldn't call me out on my hand positioning. Instead, she kept quiet, was respectful, and then we moved on.

I really appreciated her silence. She didn't interfere or assume she knew how to help me. She just let me be. That moment was crucial in our relationship. I began to trust her and felt safe to figure things out on my own, asking her questions, all while making plenty of mistakes. Looking back, I know she was inspired, teaching me what she could, and letting me figure things out on my own. Learning to read music opened a door for me that influenced my songwriting ability tremendously.

I started writing songs when I was eleven years old. I was already an avid journal writer for three years. Most journal entries had a one-line description of the day's highlight declaring I had just woken up or eaten something yummy followed with a goodbye. As my interest in music grew, so did my writing. Many of my early writings have long been forgotten except one. It was the one that I had put to a melody and it brought my writing alive.

For Christmas one year, my parents bought me a karaoke machine. It had a microphone, cassette player, and AM/FM radio. My dad had tons of cassette tapes, and I would take his tapes and record songs from the radio on my machine. I sang along to the radio and would imagine myself as the singer. I spent countless hours listening to those songs, studying its lyrical content, melodies, and harmonies. It was even better when their music video was on TV. We would record it on our VHS tapes and learn the dance routines. I always loved anything from Mariah Carey. I also liked listening to girl and boy bands and tried to perform their songs and dance choreography from their music videos. The Backstreet Boys and the Spice Girls were big at that time.

In sixth grade, my friends and I were talking about music and all the artists we liked during lunch. We started talking about the Spice Girls and debated over who we thought was the best Spice Girl. I don't remember how we got to this point but we decided it would be a great idea to throw a Spice Girl concert. My friend Ashley was the only one willing to be a Spice Girl with me. We tried convincing our other friends to join us, but they didn't want to, so it was left to me and Ashley to do the concert. Our other friends, Eme, Suli, and Kerissa, helped us instead with our planning. We decided to have the concert during our last recess that day. We quickly decided on things we needed to get done for the concert. We needed a location for a stage, we needed to make tickets to give to our friends, we needed ushers to show people their seats, and we needed bodyguards to protect us.

We planned to have our concert right outside my classroom. My classroom was outside in a portable. After finishing my lunch, I went straight to my classroom to ask my teacher if I could borrow her tape. She gave me some and I went to the south side of the portable and started taping the ground to show where the stage was and taped in rows for the audience. A few kids asked me what I was doing and I explained to them about the concert and invited them to come next recess. They didn't seem as excited about it as I was. My friend Kerissa asked some of our taller classmates to be bodyguards. Ashley and I went to the classroom to make some tickets. We ripped some paper into small squares and started handing them out to anyone and everyone we saw explaining to them what they were for. The bell rang and we had to get back to class.

Class time seemed longer than usual as I sat there frequently looking at the clock. I was excited and couldn't wait to have the concert. As it came close to recess time, I was getting nervous. The moment the bell rang, I was the first one out of the classroom. Kerissa had kids line up to the tape we decided was the entrance. There were about five kids in line when we decided it was time to let them in and seat them. Eme and Suli were the ushers and showed them where to sit. As they got to their seats, we waited a little longer in case more kids would show up. After five minutes, no one did, so we started our concert.

Ashley started by singing her favorite song at the time by her favorite singer Celine Dion, "My Heart Will Go On." She did a great job. It was now our turn to do "Wannabe" by the

Spice Girls. By this time there was only three people left, Eme, Suli, and Kerissa. Ashley and I were getting ready to perform when the bell rang. I was disappointed my planning went down the drain. We didn't even get to perform yet. Was I overzealous? Everyone started lining up and entered their classrooms and I was left kicking rocks and pebbles on my stage singing to myself, "So tell me what you want, what you really, really want. I wanna, I wanna, I wanna . . ." That was the first and last time I organized my own concert.

With my dad's musical influence in my life, my mom's influence is different. She's a tough lady. She made sure I knew my hands were no excuse from trying new things, and I'm grateful she pushed me to try new things. Growing up, I saw her create many things with her hands. She said she learned from watching her own mother and advised me to watch her. She would be knitting or crocheting something. She made many beautiful blankets and quilts. She made them for our home, sold them, or gave them away as gifts. She made special blankets for each of us kids. She taught me and any of my siblings who were interested to knit and crochet simple things like a scarf or hat. Thanks to that skill, I've been able to make many scarves and hats as gifts. My mom is a seamstress by profession and sewed me many clothes and dresses for special occasions or whenever she wanted us to be in matching outfits.

When I was a teenager, my mom let me use her sewing machine. In eighth grade, I wanted to make myself my own pair of bell bottom pants. They were in style at the time and I only had one stylish pair of bell bottoms that had a flower applique on my right hip. They were my favorite jeans and I would wear them two to even three times a week. Since my parents couldn't afford to buy me more clothes, I thought to make me another pair of bell bottoms.

My mom had a bin filled with different fabric patterns. I found me some cute blue floral fabric. I was really excited and got the sewing machine threaded and ready to go. I started measuring and cutting the fabric to the pattern of my favorite pair of jeans. As I sewed the seams together, I started imagining how my pants were going to look on me the next day. I thought of my friends and how impressed they would be with my skills. When I finished, I tried them on and thankfully they fit me. They were a bit tight on my thighs, but I was able to walk in them. I was excited and eager for school the next day.

The next morning, I woke up extra early and got ready for school. Feeling great about my pants, I was beaming with confidence that morning and walked with a pep in my step as I head to my first class that day: art. Entering the classroom, I set my bag down at my desk and grabbed my art project in the back of the room. We were painting tiles. I set my tile on my desk and sat waiting for class to start. Admiring my pants, I was amazed at how great they felt. *I did a really good job sewing my pants*, I thought to myself. *I should make me more pants and even other clothes. These pants feel even better today than they did last night. They're not even tight!*

Class began and five minutes into my teacher's opening lecture, I felt a breeze on my inner right thigh. *Whoa! Where did that come from?* Looking around me trying to find the source of this breeze, I didn't have a clue. The door was closed. There were no windows in the classroom. I thought it might be the air conditioning coming through the vents. Nope. No vents were near me. Another breeze. I looked down at my thigh and there it was, a hole. My pant leg had ripped at the seams. I started panicking trying to figure out a way to cover the hole. I had no extra pair of pants to change into, but I did have a thin jacket in my backpack I could tie around my waist. I grabbed my jacket from my backpack and asked to be excused to the bathroom.

Rushing in to the bathroom, there was no one there thankfully. I took my jacket off to see the damages in the mirror. I could not believe what I was seeing. The tear from my thigh went three inches up my behind. *Dang! Have I been walking all morning with this tear? Did everyone see my underwear?* I thought. *No wonder my pants felt so great today. How embarrassing!*

For the rest of that day, I had my jacket tied around my waist and kept a close watch on the hole. I didn't want it to rip any more than it already had. Funny thing is I went home and tried fixing the hole. I closed the hole on the sewing machine and tried the pants on again. They no longer fit me. I sewed too much and made the pants smaller. I never made pants again, but I did try making other things.

I made matching miniskirts for my three cousins and me. My cousin got us some cute pink fabric. I went home that day excited and confident in my sewing skills. *These skirts are going to turn out great*, I thought. However, I failed to get their body measurements and went home sewing blindly. Sewing taught me how important it is to make a plan and pattern to follow before executing a project.

With these few examples, I learned more about myself as I pursued these different interests. I discovered what I was good at, what I was bad at, and what I felt was worth giving my time and effort to improve on. The joy and satisfaction I felt motivated me to continue on my pursuit of these interests which grew into skills and talents I have used to help others. My advice is to explore your interests. Try new things. Even if it's random or unexpected of you, you'll never know unless you give it a try. Plus, you'll never know where it might lead you or to whom it might lead you to.

Sometimes I find myself thinking, *What would've happened if I had let my hands get in the way and never pursued the piano? What if I had ignored how I felt while playing the piano?* I know I would not be the person that I am today. I wouldn't know what I am capable of. And I know I wouldn't be living up to my potential or feel fulfillment in my life. So, I ask you to find what moves you. What fills your heart with joy? What itches your soul, so to speak, and leaves you no other choice but to get that itch out? *This* is the workings of God's Spirit awakening your spirit. Only God knows who you truly are because He knew you before you came to earth (see Jeremiah 1:5). He created you. We each come to earth to rediscover Him and His goodness in our lives by how we live; by how we perform our song.

CHAPTER 3

Creating Harmony

Harmony is my favorite part of music. What amazes me most about harmony is how two or more different notes put together can create beautiful music. Its sole purpose is to celebrate and unite differences together. Just like musical harmony, we each seek harmony in our own lives whether it's in the home, school, or work. We tend to gravitate towards familiarity avoiding any dissimilarities within our surroundings.

The world teaches us to act, talk, and even be a certain way which can diminish our self-confidence when we don't measure up or can't quite get things right. But have you ever thought that God made you different on purpose? I've thought about it many times. Why do we all have to be so different? Why do I look like this and not like everyone else? Why can't I be like the pretty girl? There's a reason why we are different, and I feel harmony plays a big part in God's divine lesson plan to teach us His ways. We've seen some of the ugliest atrocities mankind has ever seen because of disharmony, but Jesus Christ strived during His earthly ministry to pave the way for a new law, a new way of serving, and a new way of loving and accepting others that the world needed then and still needs today.

The hardest part about harmony is combining these differences together. It's understanding how important and necessary each part is to create beautiful music. For example, it may seem impossible to find harmony with that one person that rubs you the wrong way, but I promise you it isn't. You need their differences just as much as they need yours. Now I'm not saying to let them walk all over you or to even endanger yourself, but it is in the differences of others you discover what makes you *you*. Consider your family. Each member is different, and as you learn to live with each other in harmony, you start to become the being God intended you to be. When we have life experiences that may challenge us, questioning who we are and what we're capable of, it's in that moment that we decide what we contribute to our surrounding harmony.

I can still remember vividly the first time my dad taught Edward, Dempsey, and me to sing a simple three-part harmony. I was nine years old, and I remember feeling so confused at first. My dad would sing to each of us our parts. Edward had the melody, which was the middle part. I had the higher harmony, and Dempsey had the lower harmony. My dad would count us in and we would start singing. It did not sound pretty, and Dempsey and I always ended up singing with Edward.

My brothers and I would joke and play around and then try to sing when Dad would count us in. After almost an hour, Dad grew impatient and grabbed the fly swatter to smack our feet if we didn't get our part. That's when we stopped playing around and seriously started trying. After many attempts, we slowly started singing our parts right. We didn't learn our parts completely that night, but with a few more practices with Dad, we eventually got the song down.

Singing harmony was cool. I was amazed at how nice it sounded with the three of us singing three different parts. It changed the quality of the song, and it changed the feelings in my heart. I was never the same after learning that simple harmony. We performed that song a couple months later at a family reunion. All I gotta say is Alvin and the Chipmunks had nothing on us. It was from this performance that we started a new family tradition and I became obsessed with harmony.

If there's one thing my family did constantly growing up, it was singing. My dad made sure that we participated in any and all church events that we could. He volunteered us to sing for community events, social gatherings, and meetings with friends and extended family relatives. Occasionally we would sing secular music, but the majority of music we sang was religious. One time, my dad had us sing a Jackson 5 medley of their hit songs dancing a simple dance routine for a party. That was the first and last time we ever attempted to dance and sing. Dancing while singing is not a talent our family shares.

Every Christmas starting when I was ten, we would go caroling. For the first few years it was a lot of fun. I especially liked eating the yummy treats people would give us during the holidays. My mom would have us dressed in matching outfits. One year, she made me and my sisters red-and-black plaid dresses with the itchy puffy-armed sleeves to match with her red sparkly top. My brothers and dad were dressed in their collared white shirts and red ties. We would sing to the sick, the widows, the elderly and disabled people, and basically anyone who was in need of some good ol' Christmas cheer.

As each one of us became teenagers, we started to dread Christmastime only because of caroling. We each took turns attempting to go on strike from caroling. The keyword is "attempt," and you're probably wondering what's so bad about caroling during Christmas time. Well, let me paint the picture for you.

My family doesn't carol like regular carolers do. Regular carolers usually go to someone's home and knock on the door, people open the door, you sing a couple songs, and then you go to the next house and do the same thing over again. We, on the other hand, never did the caroling at the doorstep approach. The way we caroled is we would start two or three days before Christmas and end two or three days *after* Christmas. We would carol for four to six days straight starting as early as 8 a.m. and end as late as midnight each day.

My dad went above and beyond to make appointments with people to carol to, and he would have a set list of people to visit every year. That list grew longer as the years went by and people started requesting us to come stop by their family Christmas party. He made sure our day was filled with people to visit and places to go.

The other reason why we couldn't do the doorstep approach is because my dad needed access to an electrical outlet for his big seventy-five-pound keyboard. As my siblings and I got older, my dad's carol repertoire became longer, and we would spend forty-five minutes to an hour in each home. In every appointment, my dad would give a short speech in the beginning, we would sing our thirty-minute set, and then my dad would end with his closing speech before we'd sing our last song and leave.

Every December, we would start practicing our carol songs a couple weeks before Christmas. We would constantly complain about not having time to stay home and relax and enjoy our Christmas, but my Dad was firm with his decision every year for us to go caroling. One year, I was determined to get out of caroling. I couldn't bear the embarrassment. What seemed cool when I was younger wasn't cool anymore, especially when you're a teenager and you happen to walk into a home of a cute boy you used to have a crush on. And it didn't help to have my dad jamming on the keyboard all while dancing his dad moves.

This happened the year before, and I didn't want to have to go through that again this year.

On our first day to carol, I was in my room trying everything I could to delay us from leaving. My mom called for me to hurry because we were going to be late to our first appointment. Sitting on my bed crying, I was angry. *Why do we have to go carol?* I thought. I heard a honk from outside. I got up to look out my window and saw that everyone was in the van waiting for me. I thought if I took my time, we would somehow miraculously stay home and not carol, but I was wrong. I knew if I continued to stay in my room I would be in big trouble with my dad and I did not want that. I grabbed my things and joined the rest of my family in the van.

I don't remember my dad ever scolding me that morning when I got into the ride. He kept silent and we left to our first appointment. During the car ride, I was so mad that I was there. I was so mad that caroling even existed. Like, who invented caroling? I was so mad that I was a part of this family. Couldn't I choose when I want to be a part of this family? Because I'd like to opt out for the next few days. For weeks leading up to Christmas week, I swore I wouldn't go caroling and, yet, there I was. So, during the car ride to our first appointment, I decided that if I had to go caroling, I might as well make it as miserable and unpleasant for everyone.

The first house we arrived late (thanks to me), but they happily invited us into their home. They were waiting for us. I ignored my parents and tried my best not to hide my contempt for them. I must've eye-rolled and mean-mugged anyone I made eye contact with, but I was only greeted with a concerned smile. *Ugh!* I thought. *Why can't you people let me be mad? I don't even want to be here!* But something magical happened that day.

With every house we went to, the anger in my heart slowly melted away and was replaced with feelings of love and joy.

As I reflect on the many times I tried rebelling and protesting caroling, those contentious feelings would quickly leave me as I would see the joy on the faces of the people we sang to. This was something each of my siblings experienced as well. Even though we still complain about the duration of our caroling days, we can't deny the hidden blessings that came from it. I used to think that my dad taught me to sing so we could be famous like his famous nieces and nephews, but the honest truth was he taught us to sing so we could serve others and uplift those with heavy hearts and troubled souls.

We've seen and felt how special our service was in the many homes we visited and caroled to. Did I hate my caroling days? Yes! But I don't regret the experience. Because my dad was consistent in teaching us to sing and providing many opportunities for us to do so, we grew close as a family and our singing reflected that. Even our harmonies sounded as one voice. We became one as a family and that translated in our daily family life.

Growing up, I was blessed with an amazing support system. I know that now. Home is where it all began, and I was very fortunate to have been raised by goodly parents who desired for us to live faithfully to God. My dad made sure that we spent as much time together supporting each other's interests as a family. We did almost everything together. If there was a way that he could include my family, my dad would have us right there with him.

My dad owned a franchise of a commercial cleaning business. He did that for more than ten years. When he first started, he would go and clean the commercial buildings by himself. Sometimes we'd all go together and he and my mom would clean while we'd be in the car sleeping waiting for them to finish. As we got older, he involved us in the cleaning and we helped them.

We cleaned all kinds of businesses, medical clinics, dental offices, banks, trade schools, and even car dealerships. My dad gave us cleaning assignments and I was the lucky one stuck with cleaning bathrooms. My dad didn't want me cleaning the bathrooms, but my mom was adamant about me doing this tough, dirty job. When someone was missing we all had to help each other out so I've had my fair share of cleaning everything.

When my brothers and I were older and could drive, we'd go cleaning on our own when my dad was unable to due to other work constraints as he was always juggling two to three jobs at a time. We would always complain about doing his cleaning job, but we were only concerned for ourselves and sleep. Many nights we would go cleaning on a school night coming home past midnight to sleep before waking up at 6 a.m. to go to school, and then we'd repeat the same process again that very night. As my siblings started participating in school sports, they got out of cleaning most of the time when they had night games or practices.

Cleaning for my family was therapeutic. Many nights we'd catch ourselves deep in conversation in the break room or in the car. We'd always have competitions. It was always fun racing my parents. It was usually a tie between me and my mom on who was the slowest. Edward was always the one to beat. We'd play games as we cleaned to make it fun, but sometimes that fun got us into trouble where we had to call 911 for help. Can you guess who we called 911 for? It was for Dempsey.

One night, Edward and Dempsey were trying to scare each other. We got to our last building of the night, and Edward and Dempsey were still at it, finding new places to hide in to scare each other. This particular building had a changing room with metal lockers. Dempsey decided to hide inside one of the lockers in hopes of scaring Edward. Dempsey searched the lockers and found one that was empty. He got inside the locker and closed the locker quietly in case Edward was nearby. What he failed to see was the padlock that was secure on the locker handle. The locker he chose was the only locker with a padlock but he assumed it was like the others.

Edward came into the room looking for Dempsey. As Edward started searching the lockers, Dempsey knew this was the perfect opportunity to jump out and scare him. As Dempsey lifted the lever from inside, he was surprised to find he could not lift it up. Revealing himself to Edward, he asked for help. Edward searched the remaining lockers and realized Dempsey had chosen the only padlocked locker. Edward teased him for a good minute before notifying our parents. When my parents came and saw the predicament Dempsey was in, they scolded him as they tried to figure out a way to get him out.

My dad went to look for something to cut the padlock, but my mom was scared for Dempsey's life that he wouldn't be able to breathe inside the locker. She decided to call 911. Within thirty minutes, firefighters came and cut the lock open. Dempsey was saved. Several weeks later while watching the morning news, we saw some firefighters being interviewed by the local news station. The news reporter asked the firefighter, "What's the most interesting call you ever received?" His response, "We recently got an interesting call of a boy who locked himself in a locker at three in the morning." He began to describe Dempsey's locker experience, and we all started laughing as we realized they were talking about Dempsey.

The cleaning business made for some unforgettable memories for my family and for cousins and friends who slept over our house. They had to come clean with us, but we always had fun and still reminisce of our cleaning days. But with the fun memories, there were also bad ones too. We had plenty of arguments, even fist fights, and cleaning helped to diffuse the anger until we got home for a family meeting. And don't get me started on family meetings. My dad seriously loves having family meetings. I'm just kidding, but it felt like that was his favorite thing to do as a family since we had them often.

Outside of our weekly FHE, my dad had us gather for family meetings on any day of the week whenever he felt prompted to. You could always expect one when someone was fighting in the home or got into trouble outside of the home. Depending on the severity of the problem, my dad would personally meet with that family member, and then he would call another family meeting after to teach and counsel us all. I never understood why he would have those frequent family meetings, but those meetings kept us close.

My dad's musical gifts influenced me the most out of all my siblings. My dad wrote songs, so I wrote songs. He played instruments, so I played instruments. My dad taught voice, so I started to teach voice. I became very interested in harmony when I turned eleven years old. Anyone who played with me knew we were going to sing. I wanted to try out different harmonies, but I wanted others to feel what I felt from singing harmony.

My first friends were my cousins and with the family reunions we had annually, we would sing whenever we'd get together. There I'd be teaching the girls to sing a song I just wrote the night before. One year, we decided to be called Island Girls 6, or IG6, because there were six of us. I'd ask each girl to sing a part, and we'd try to harmonize. Because I was brutally honest in correcting them, they started getting frustrated with me and would leave to go play somewhere else. By this time there were only four of us, and we changed our name to IGX or Island Girls Extreme because we thought that sounded cooler. We fantasized of making it big with our pink skirts. Remember those pink miniskirts I tried to make? Well, we tried to look the part, sound the part, and even dance the part. It was fun while it lasted for that summer.

From junior high to high school, I became really close to Eme and Mele. Eme and I are related and have always been close since we were babies. She was my childhood best friend. Her temperament was different from mine. She was quiet, amicable, good-natured, and genuinely kindhearted. We were like yin and yang. Our relationship translated through our singing and we blended so well when we'd sing in harmony.

Eme and I knew Mele since elementary school, and honestly, I never thought we'd ever become friends. She wasn't a member of the Church like Eme and I were, so I didn't see her on Sundays. She and her family are faithful members of the Methodist faith, and I occasionally saw her when my family went to support my aunty, who was also a member of their congregation. The only thing I thought we had in common was our Tongan culture, living in the same neighborhood, and attending the same schools together.

One day in junior high, Eme and I were waiting for our ride home since we carpooled together. We started singing (like we always did) Destiny's Child's newest hit at the time, "Say My Name." Mele was waiting for her ride too, and overhearing us sing, she decided to join in on our song. She had a great alto voice, and we were having a lot of fun singing together. When our rides came, I was sad to stop singing and we made plans to get together again the next day. We started singing a lot together. We looked for opportunities to sing at school, each other's churches, or community functions.

Eme and I got to know Mele better as we spent time with her in her home. Despite our different faiths, I realized her family was no different from mine. I always felt loved whenever I was at Mele's house. I sometimes wonder how things would've been if we never sang that day. I would've never known the joy her friendship would bring me in my life. I would've never felt the support I would desperately need from her during some of the most difficult times in my life. I never would've gained one of my bestest friends.

You know how there's that one person in school who always sings the National Anthem? That was me. Any chance I could I would include Eme and Mele to sing with me. We learned different arrangements for the National Anthem and we tried them out each time we sang. I was lucky to have them and their support. Every performance we had was different and affected our friendship in some way. Sometimes we'd mess up the words or forget our parts, other times we'd do great, and a few times were just embarrassingly funny.

Tripping and falling was always embarrassing, but I'll never forget an experience I had at a varsity basketball game. I was asked to sing the national anthem earlier that day by a basketball player and assumed it was for the basketball game later that day. I found out a little too late that it was not for that game. Eme, Mele, and I arrived late to the game and only had fifteen minutes to practice until game time. We quickly practiced once before the start of the game. We've sung the national anthem often for various sporting events that it became habit to enter into the gym when they would announce the national anthem. So, we waited for our cue just outside the entrance doors of the gym.

As we heard the announcer announce, "Please rise for the National Anthem," Eme, Mele, and I started walking into the gym to sing. I entered first and was determined to get to the microphone as quickly as possible. As I got to the middle of the basketball court, I heard some girl sing, "Oh, say can you see." I was surprised. I thought I was supposed to sing. I didn't see anyone at the mic. I gradually felt all eyes turn to my direction as every step I took sounded louder and louder.

I soon realized the singer was none other than a recording of Whitney Houston. I thought to stop and face the flag, but I was too embarrassed to stop. I looked behind me and saw that Eme and Mele were nowhere to be found. They were able to escape the embarrassment and had only walked a few steps before hearing Whitney's voice when they turned back around. We laugh now, but I learned my lesson to never make assumptions and to be sure to confirm. Talk about *moded* ("moded" is a slang term that most Polynesians use for being "proven wrong in an embarrassing manner"[1]).

There were times where our singing helped us resolve problems we had with each other. We loved singing together so much that we always found a way to resolve our differences. When the Winter Olympics came to Salt Lake City, Utah, in 2002, our school counselor Carol Goulais gave us many opportunities to sing and perform at several venues in downtown Salt Lake City. I included in our set an original song of mine I wrote a few years prior, and we needed a fourth person to sing the arrangement I made. I invited my first cousin Luisa to sing with us. Luisa joining us changed our sound, so we had extra practices to fine tune our sound and tighten our harmonies.

We had to start over and find a balance in our harmonies. We eventually got our parts right, but even that didn't improve our sound because we still didn't click as friends. Our first day singing together was rough. We'd never performed together until then and it was apparent in our performance. I was feeling discouraged after our first day and I was ready to give up. It wasn't until we all had a heart-to-heart conversation that I felt hopeful we'd do better and thankfully we did. When a new change occurs, it can cause some distress to the current flow of things, but through consistent hard work things do improve if you desire it. We did all we could to prepare musically for our performance, but it was in strengthening our relationship that made all the difference in our song.

It's so important that you choose your friends wisely. The people you surround yourself with will either build you up or tear you down. It's the friends who stick through the good and the ugly, who remain loyal, who reminds you of your worth when you forget it yourself that you want to keep close to you always. I consider myself a friendly person, but my circle of close friends has always been small. I'm very fortunate to have friends who I know without a doubt would never give up on me—even when I gave up on myself.

With all these experiences I had with my family and friends, I had to learn how to coexist in harmony with them. This strengthened our relationships with one another. We basically learned how to be different—together. And even when there were times where things became disharmonious, my father instilled in me the importance of living in harmony with God. Living in harmony with God's teachings enables me to live in harmony with others developing a more tolerant outlook on life. Doing so brought feelings of peace, joy, and contentment in my life and in my home.

NOTE

1. Urban Dictionary, s.v. "moded," https://www.urbandictionary.com /define.php?term=moded.

CHAPTER 4

Finding the Rhythm

Rhythm is the heartbeat of music. It is defined as having a regular and repeated pattern of movement or sound. Without it, music would not have the impact it has especially combined with other musical elements. It sets the pace and is the constant guide you can depend on to always find your way back even when you go astray. Rhythmically speaking, there are three things that have always remained constant in my life: God, music, and my disability.

Ever since I could remember, we always went to church. It was mandatory, no questions asked. The only reason that would keep any of us from attending church was illness, but no matter where we were in the world we always attended church. Our church membership was in a Tongan-speaking ward, so every Sunday we attended all our church meetings and any activities throughout the week. There was always something happening in our ward or in our stake. I have so many fond memories attending dances, enjoying many activities at camp, and participating in countless devotionals and firesides. Anything our ward did, we participated in it.

The Church highly influenced our lives and everything we did. I watched my parents faithfully serve in their church callings, always going above and beyond to help those within their stewardships, and incorporating their faith in our family life. We read scriptures as a family. Even before I could read, I would sit with my parents and listen to them as they would read together. They gave me my own book to make me feel included and even let me pretend to read. They got a kick out of listening to me make up my own scripture stories when it was my turn to read.

Since scripture study was important, so was prayer. Family prayer was mandatory and many of our family meetings happened before family prayer. When my parents worked in the mornings, my dad was adamant about me and my siblings saying prayer together before leaving home to go to school. I can't count how many times my dad would counsel us to say our prayers morning and night. We couldn't go to sleep without saying family prayer at night. Many times, my brothers would fall asleep and my dad would wake them up to join us in family prayer. I learned quickly it is better that we call for family prayer when we got tired than take our chances and be woken up.

My parents did their best to teach us about God by the example they set. They also knew by actively living our faith, we would experience the power of God in our lives and we did. Some things they had us do was memorize the Articles of Faith by the time we turned twelve. Because we couldn't watch TV on Sunday, it was the perfect day for us to memorize them. My parents would send us to our rooms to memorize one of the Articles of Faith, and we weren't allowed to come out until we were ready to recite whichever Article of Faith we were memorizing at the time. It became a race for my brothers and me.

We had weekly Family Home Evenings (FHE) on Sunday or Monday nights depending on my parents' work schedules. We had opportunities to teach each other during FHE. My dad would assign us the week before—or sometimes the day of—to prepare a lesson for FHE. I particularly hated being asked the day of. During FHE, we could always count on my dad to go around the room and ask each of us to share what we learned in church the previous day. Sometimes I'd forget what I learned, and I'd either make up something about Jesus or just admit I forgot and get lectured about listening.

As I got older, I was curious about why my dad always asked us about what we learned in church and finally asked him about it. "Dad, why did you always ask us about what we learned in church? Did you want to know if we were listening?" My dad thoughtfully responded, "I didn't ask you to see if you were listening. I asked you to see if you were being taught." That left a deep impression in my heart, and I was slowly starting to understand my dad's craziness.

We also had a tradition to bear our testimony in fast and testimony meeting on our birthday month. My mom and Dempsey share the same birthday month with me, so Dempsey and I would play the waiting game to go up to share our testimony. Dempsey and I would glance at each other daring the other to go first. My mom would glare at us if we got too loud, and if we were close enough, she'd pinch us to be quiet. We'd purposely sit far away from her on that Sunday. But I'd always have a smile of relief after I'd share my testimony. I was one of those kids who would recite a memorized testimony my parents taught me. It was in those moments of bearing testimony that I was learning and discovering my own testimony.

When I was fifteen years old, my dad made the decision to move my family from the Tongan-speaking ward to the English-speaking ward. We had a family meeting when my dad announced about the move to us. We asked him why and all he could say was, "The move is for you guys. You'll understand someday." My brothers and I were upset. I was frustrated with his reason and wanted to understand right at that moment. His main concern was that we were not understanding what was taught in the Tongan language, and the truth was he was right. We didn't understand Tongan. Tongan was the first language I spoke, but when I started going to school I started speaking more English than Tongan. As my siblings and I got older, my parents spoke more English than Tongan too, and English became the main language we used to communicate at home.

I particularly was not fond of listening to my dad's broken English when he was lecturing one or all of us. He had a habit of repeating the same thing over and over again, each time wording it different as if its meaning would change, but nope. He was saying the same thing differently, and we would slowly zone out which would cause him to continue on repeating himself until he felt we understood him. But as my parents started speaking more English than Tongan, we slowly started losing the Tongan language. Edward, Dempsey, and I understand more Tongan than my younger three siblings due to the fact that we were exposed more to the Tongan language than they were.

This decision to move from the Tongan ward was sudden too. I thought my dad would give us time, but he only gave us a week's notice. I remember the Sunday following our family meeting would be our last Sunday in the Tongan ward. We met with the bishop as a family. I vividly remember all eight of us entering the bishop's office. He shook each of our hands and we all took a seat. My parents and the bishop shared small talk and then bishop asked my dad what he could do for us. As my dad said, "Bishop, we are moving to the *palangi* ward," I'll never forget the bishop's surprised look on his face. "Palangi" is the Tongan word for white. The bishop naturally asked why and my dad shared his concerns for us, his children. He asked us to stay several times, but my dad was firm with his decision and the bishop respectfully accepted it and wished us well in our new ward.

Everyone in my family wanted to stay in the Tongan ward except my dad. Now, don't get me wrong. Attending the Tongan ward blessed my family in so many ways, but my dad's decision to move us was inspired. At the time, it didn't feel like a blessing. I enjoyed going to church to socialize with the friends I made there, but the honest truth was I really had no interest in learning the gospel. It was evident when I'd be in class with my peers and I would seek to be the center of attention by making loud, disruptive comments in hopes to get others to laugh and notice me. I was that kid who was disrespectful even to the teacher and, shamefully, I admit, I even made one of my Sunday School teachers cry. I didn't care about others' feelings but my own, and I did my best to appear invincible.

I participated in church activities only because that was what everyone did and what my parents taught me to do. But the honest truth is I did not have a personal testimony of the gospel or of Jesus Christ besides the one my parents taught me to recite when I was a Primary-aged child. I liked church only because of the people who were there, and I tried my best to fit in and even impress them. My dad must've sensed the spiritual danger I was in and made the courageous decision to move.

The following Sunday, we attended our neighborhood ward. I'll never forget the first Sunday. As we walked in, I noticed the ward was very diverse in ethnicity and age. I saw some kids I went to school with there. I saw a few neighbors who lived down the street from us whom I hadn't known were members of the Church. I was not happy to be there and was convinced that this ward was the lamest ward we'd ever been to. The real reason I opposed this move was the fact that I hate being the new kid, having to start all over, making new friends, and proving myself again that I'm more than some helpless disabled girl.

When we attended classes in our new ward, the youth size was a third of the size as the Tongan ward. I had a hard time with that, especially since up to this point I only liked going to church to socialize. Because of the smaller class sizes, I had no distractions. The class setting was more intimate, and the teacher really could reach and teach each of us individually. I basically couldn't hide anymore. I had no choice but to listen and try to make sense of what was being taught, and if I was lost my teacher knew and would always address any concerns I had in their lesson.

With regular church attendance, my dad made sure there were constantly music opportunities for our family in and out-side of the church. I've shared some of what my dad did musi-cally for my family outside of the church, but within the church it was no different. Any time my family spoke in sacrament meeting, we'd always include two to three musical numbers. I always liked doing musical numbers because it meant shorter talks for everyone.

Since I can remember, my dad was involved with music in every ward we've ever been in. One year, my dad got called to be the ward choir director in our palangi ward. The first choir practice my dad had, I can count how many people showed up on my hands—and that's on one hand. So, my dad had my family join the choir and we ended up being the ward choir. I laugh because it was just us and maybe three other people. Our harmonies were tight even though we were small in numbers. My dad would have me help out by playing the piano. I enjoyed playing and learned a lot just from following him as he directed the choir.

As I watched my dad sing a lot in trios and quartets and in his band, I would try to do the same. The only thing I did do more often than my father was sing solos. The first time I performed my first solo was when I was eight years old. It was during the ward's Primary program, and I sang the Primary song, "Where Love Is." I was wearing a beautiful white dress and performed it during the morning rehearsals. When it came time for me to sing in the program, I couldn't sing a single word and cried from beginning to end. I was terrified.

In time, I got better with each opportunity my father provided for me, and I was able to overcome my fear of singing in public without succumbing to tears. Of all the places I ever sang in, it always felt like home singing in the church. I was slowly building my self-confidence, exploring my capabilities, and discovering my own testimony of Christ with each performance. Family and friends started requesting for me to do a solo, and I happily obliged. The opportunity that impacted me the most was when I would sing with the Moleni Brothers.

The Moleni Brothers are the sons of Fisi and Liahona Moleni. Six of their seven sons sang in this group. They immigrated to the United States from New Zealand in the '90s. We used to attend the same Tongan ward and they would often sing in sacrament meeting. I was always blown away by their talent and compared them to Boyz II Men. They would put on musical firesides or devotionals locally in Utah, out of state, and even out of the country. When I was fifteen years old, they started inviting me to sing in their firesides. I always enjoyed their firesides because I felt uplifted listening to their testimonies through spoken word and especially through song. The strength of their brotherhood was evident in their singing and it impacted all those who heard them sing, myself included.

On one occasion, they invited me to help them out with a fireside they were doing in the Salt Lake Valley. I agreed to help, but was conflicted because they wanted me to speak and share my testimony. Up to this point, I always sang a song or two in their firesides and that was it. Fisi Jr. was persistent and asked me to share my testimony, but I refused several times until finally I consented. The honest truth was I didn't feel I had a strong enough testimony of Christ and about the gospel. I knew I had one somewhere deep inside me, but I was still trying to find it myself. I was struggling at the time with the one constant in my life I questioned and even detested its existence: my hands.

We are all born into this world different and unique. I was no exception. I had a fun childhood and have some of the greatest memories any child could have. I didn't feel any different from those around me even though I did things differently. I was able to accomplish and do things like everyone else did. You often don't realize your differences until you start comparing yourself to others. It's natural to compare yourself. We all do it. We can't help but do it to see what is best for us or to see where we fit in. But it's interesting how people can make you feel inferior sometimes without even knowing it.

Junior high school was challenging. On my first day of seventh grade, I experienced a roller coaster of emotions. During the car ride to school, I couldn't help but miss my five younger siblings, especially since we'd been going to the same school for the past six years. This year was Ekuasi's first year going to school as a new kindergartner. He was lucky he had everyone with him except me. I was nervous to be in a new school without them.

Sitting there, missing them, I tried to imagine what school would be like and would replay scenes from the TV show *Saved by the Bell* in my mind. We pulled up to school fifteen minutes early. My parents were just as nervous for me as I was since this was their first time experiencing junior high too, and in America for that matter. Dad wished me luck on my first day and said he'd be back to pick me up from school later. As I got out of my van, my heart was racing from nerves and excitement. I can still remember the smell of damp, freshly cut grass as I walked into the school. Taking a look around I had two thoughts: I needed to get to my locker and I needed to find Eme.

The hallways were busy with all kinds of kids—older kids. I no longer was the older kid. Oh, how I felt so small walking down that hallway toward my locker. I got to my locker and pulled out the piece of paper that had the combination to open my lock. I only opened my locker once at orientation, but somehow I couldn't open my locker this time. I didn't want to be obvious but I was feeling scared inside as my thoughts began to race.

I'm in a new school. I don't know what I'm doing. I don't even know if this is my locker. I swear this is my locker. Did I do the combination right? I want to go home. Deep breath! Try again. Stay calm. Look like you know what you're doing, or they'll notice.

And then it opened.

Ring!

The first bell rang.

Great, I thought. *Just when I opened it, I have to get to class. I didn't even find Eme yet. I hope she's all right.*

My first period was French. As I entered the classroom, I recognized a few familiar faces. That was a relief. But making my way to a desk to sit in, I couldn't help but feel so out of place. There was so much to take in with this new schedule and different classrooms to go to each hour. I was trying my best to keep my composure, but deep down inside I was trying not to cry. I missed my old school, and I especially missed recess.

That first day of school was longer than what I was used to. It was boring. All we did in each class was sit and listen to each teacher lecture. Each class I would hope to find one of my friends in there, but it was cool seeing and meeting new people who I felt could potentially be my friends. I later found Eme in the hallway on my way to my last class. I was so happy to see her and we briefly spoke for a little bit before leaving to our next period. Lunchtime became my favorite part of the day. I qualified for free lunch, and I loved the fact that I could make a choice on what I wanted to eat, especially since the food I ate at school were things we usually didn't eat at home.

Up until this week, I never paid attention to the stares. I started to recognize how uncomfortable I felt when I caught people staring at me, but it was more than just staring. I would catch people staring and pointing toward me as they would whisper and even talk loud enough for me to hear them say to their neighbor, "Look at her hands!" I tried my best not to let it get to me, but it slowly started to like it never had before. This was when I started recognizing how different I looked compared to others. As a child, I hardly recognized people were staring at my hands, and if I did see them staring, I thought they were admiring my awesomeness. I was that confident because my mom continually reminded me of how special I was, but this was different. No one knew me and what I was capable of. I felt judged, belittled, and misunderstood. I wanted to be given a chance.

With the stares also came the questions. That was very difficult to deal with, and it slowly chipped away at my self-esteem. The number-one question I'd get asked was, "What happened to your hands?" and followed-up by the second-most asked question, "Did you have an accident?" I remember always getting asked these questions since I was a child, and never thought twice as I'd answer them. "Who took your fingers? Did you cut your fingers off? Why is your arm crooked?" or "Hey, why do you have short arms?" I actually appreciated the questions—well, most of them anyway. I understood people were curious, and I at times preferred the questions even if they were off the wall rather than the stares and assumptions.

Something else that is awkward, even to this day, is shaking hands. Everyone shakes hands with their right hand, but I am a lefty and feel even more uncomfortable using my right hand. It was very difficult at first because I tried to avoid a handshake with anyone and would only shake hands if the handshake was extended to me. I learned early on teenagers don't mean to be cruel, but they unintentionally can be. On several occasions, I would be offered a handshake and as I would accept and shake hands, they'd quickly remove their hand from mine, rubbing their hand in disbelief at what they just felt. Some even shrieked in surprise, terror, and even disgust for touching me. They vocalized it, and it hurt me deeply every time. I became wary of the handshake and had to learn to read the person if they really would shake my hand or not.

Unfortunately, I still feel that awkwardness today with a handshake. Who would've thought something so simple as a handshake would have such an impact on someone? Today, I play it by ear every time I greet people, because I learned early on some people are just not ready for something or someone different from them and they just don't know how to react. I can't count how many times I would extend my hand out to shake hands, and they'd look at my hand then look at me and smile awkwardly as they'd say hello leaving my hand outstretched and alone. That was big-time moded for me, but I've gotten used to it for the most part. If you're ever around me, pay attention to that. And if you ever greet me or someone like me, don't be scared to shake hands unless their whole arm is missing. In that case, you'll just have to wave hello.

The last thing that really cut deep for me were the pity remarks. So many times people would thoughtlessly say, "I feel so sorry for you. That's so sad your hands are like that." This was all new for me to hear and experience. *What's so wrong about my hands?* I would wonder. I've never felt sad about my hands before. This is all I know. Up to this point I never thought twice about my hands and how people felt about it. Hearing, seeing, and experiencing these things frequently disrupted my rhythm. It slowly started affecting me and my self-confidence, and I started to grow insecure of myself questioning my self-worth as a young teenager.

In a song, a constant rhythm can change to an irregular rhythmic pattern to show variety and interest. I was starting to experience an irregular rhythmic pattern in my life. I was not used it. I didn't like it and I tried to get back to the rhythm I was familiar with. Because I have a strong and proud personality, I tried my best to hide my insecurities by being extra everything. I was never the quiet and shy type; I was that loud, obnoxious girl in the school hallways always seeking to lead the pack and to be the center of attention. I thought if I was outgoing, sociable, and outspoken, no one would figure out that I was starting to feel unsure of myself. It was the perfect facade that masked the inner turmoil I began to battle with, or so I thought.

I did my best to act like I was happy and actively tried to be outgoing. I wanted to show that I wasn't some weak disabled girl, but that I was more than capable of doing anything. So, I sought out different activities that would best showcase my capabilities. I participated in after-school clubs. I didn't play on any sports teams except in PE class, but I always looked forward to participating in any music and singing activities.

Something the Poly kids did in school was have song battles. We'd have a boys-against-girls challenge, and because I was very confident in my singing abilities, I always sought to participate in any challenge. Most of these challenges I would initiate. I'd get my girls and we'd practice our harmonies and then we'd meet at the designated time and place to sing our songs. I honestly don't remember who won, probably because I always felt I won every time.

Most of the time we'd sing during lunch, and one of my favorite things to do is sing with new people. In eighth grade, I met a seventh grader named Mycal during lunch. The first question I asked him was, "Do you sing?" He responded timidly, "Yes." So, I made him sing for me and he did. Mycal had a great voice and I was excited to find a new friend—a singing friend, at that. Mycal and I became really good friends throughout the years because of music.

My seventh-grade year, I didn't sign up for any music classes, so I made sure I signed up for them my eighth-grade year. I chose to sing in the school choir. The choir teacher, Ms. Straussberg, was very talented, and she made class interesting and engaging, but the one thing that made an impact on me and possibly redirected my musical aspirations was her passion for music. My first day in her class, I sat with the altos. I have always wanted to sing with altos and attempted to sit with them, but after she evaluated me, I sang with the sopranos. Funny thing is, even after that year, I would always attempt to sing with the altos in any choir I sang in, but I always failed and ended up being a soprano. I coveted the alto part because my lower range was weaker than my higher range, and I really wanted to work on it and improve.

Every class period, she would be at the piano the majority of the time leading and teaching us. As she played the piano, she would give us our cue to start singing, and then I'd witness it. She'd zone in on the song, focused, and without fail she just knew when a part was off and even when someone wasn't singing. I'd be startled each time she'd slam the piano cover down, look at us, and demand our best. I would be amazed at her listening skills and wondered how she knew where we were lacking. She would cue us in again and I would feel it, her strong desire to tell the song's story right.

One day, she asked for potential soloists to audition for a part in a song we had been practicing. I really wanted to do it, but I didn't know if I could measure up to her standards and I chickened out. I sorely regretted that, and the following year I made sure that I wouldn't pass up an opportunity to audition. The following year, she asked for soloists and, feeling more confident in meeting her expectations, I auditioned for the part and got it. It was validating to be chosen for the solo.

With every singing performance I had, my confidence grew and I auditioned more. The year my school announced its school play was going to be Annie, I convinced Eme and Mele to audition with me for the part of the Boylan Sisters. Fortunately for us, we were the only ones who auditioned and got the part by default. This gave us another excuse to hang out more and sing. Opening night, we nervously sang, "You're Never Fully Dressed without a Smile." Performing on the stage was such a freeing experience, and I felt so relieved to only have to be on stage for ten minutes before we had to get off for the next scene.

I loved singing, and I loved how I felt each time I performed. But the crazy thing is as I craved the feeling and adrenaline performing gave me, I began to grow uncomfortable with people staring at my hands as I performed. I felt confused. How could I purposely put myself out there and draw all this attention to myself when deep down inside I felt scared? I was scared of first impressions, of what others would think of me. I was scared of being seen. I was scared of those *curious* questions. I was scared of the expectations and particularly the expected failure. I was scared to be me. The rhythm I had been marching to had been changed, and I was struggling to adjust to this new beat.

CHAPTER 5

Dissonance

*D*issonance = *a tension or clash resulting from two disharmonious or unsuitable elements.*[1] When I learned about dissonance in my music theory class, it made perfect sense to me. Dissonance is a problem waiting to be solved. The key word is *waiting.* I still remember my teacher playing on the piano an example of dissonance. He sat for a good five minutes playing dissonant chords without resolving them. After three minutes, it became irritating. I was ready to go to the piano and resolve his issues. But I'll never forget when he finally resolved those dissonant chords feeling a great sense of relief, peace, and satisfaction. If that was my teacher's goal to have me feel that, then he succeeded. It made me think of the dissonance in my life and the things I was still waiting to resolve.

My personal dissonance was the conflict I struggled with daily inside: to be seen or not to be seen, that was the question. Despite having to deal with constant stares, questions, and pity remarks all through my seventh grade, I was excited for eighth grade. But in eighth grade, I became more self-conscious of my hands. I started to hide my hands. Whenever I was in public, I would put my hands behind my back or in my pockets. If I was walking with my friends, I'd try my best to walk close to them to conceal my hands. Now that I think about it, I don't know how I was able to do that, but I was determined to hide my hands. In school, I'd always wear my backpack in front of me and place my hands between my backpack and my stomach.

I started wearing long-sleeved clothes regardless of the time of year. Winter time became my favorite season. When summertime rolled around, there I'd be in my sweater or jacket in ninety-degree weather. One summer day, we went to Jordan Park in Salt Lake City so my dad could play tennis. My dad loves the sport and has always been playing since I can remember. I have many memories of playing at the park as dad would play and even compete in local tennis tournaments. That day I forgot to put on a sweater, so I refused to leave the van.

My mom let me stay as they went to watch my dad play. I felt relieved, but as I sat there in the van, I began to hate the fact that I was there. If only I could go and play with my siblings on the playground. I imagined the fun I could've been having on the swings had I remembered my sweater. Soon after that, my mom came and kicked me out of the van because she said it was a waste of gas to keep the A/C on. As I walked out looking at the ground, I felt naked. My hands were exposed and I was fresh meat. I dared not to look up or notice any stares, and I definitely wasn't in the mood to answer any questions.

I felt confident as long as my hands were covered because I could avoid the unnecessary attention no matter where I was. At school, there was only one class I dreaded, and that was PE. Don't get me wrong, PE class was always fun, but wearing a long-sleeved top was uncomfortable. It was extremely hot, but I didn't want to take a chance. I did my best to act as if the heat didn't bother me and be as socially outgoing as I could even if I was sweating from wearing a sweater in the dry heat. I needed to act as if I was okay and that I really wanted to wear these sweaters and jackets, but my glistening sweaty forehead fooled nobody but me.

After school one day, my brother Edward asked me, "Why do you hide your hands?"

"What do you mean?" I responded.

"It's obvious you're trying to hide it. Even my friends were asking why you do that."

I was taken aback with his question and didn't know how to respond. For the first time, this reality I had created for myself cracked. I went to my room and was stuck in my thoughts trying to process my brother's words.

Wait! They noticed? I swear I was hiding my hands well. They were hidden in my clothes. Was I making it too obvious? When I put my hands like this (I put my hands behind my back), *it's not that noticeable, right?*

Standing in front of the mirror, I looked long and hard at myself, studying how I could make it look like I wasn't hiding my hands but still hide my hands. I was determined to hide my hands and be normal like everyone else or at least look normal like everyone else. I tried positioning my hands differently and realized no matter what I did, it was obvious. My arms are too short so you know my hands are not normal. I ignored that fact and focused on making sure I wore clothes that covered my hands.

The real reason why I was so determined to appear normal was because I experienced my first real crush that year and really wanted him to notice me. He was the new kid at school, and I was smitten from the moment I saw him. He was so cute. He was Tongan so we saw him on Sundays in the Tongan ward too. That was a plus for me because that meant I could see him six days of the week. From that moment, all the slow jams and love songs that I really liked listening to took on a whole different meaning. Every time I saw him, I would get so nervous and my heart would beat fast. I seriously couldn't breathe. This was so brand new for me, especially since I didn't understand fully what I was experiencing. Even when I snuck a glimpse at him getting a drink of water at the water fountain, I kid you not, time slowed down for real. It was pretty crazy now that I think about it, but he was the business.

My feelings for this guy were getting too much for me to handle, so much so that I actually wrote a song about it and that song won me a singing competition. I never told my best friends about this crush because I was embarrassed. When I wrote about him in my journal, I couldn't write his real name so I gave him a girl's name just in case if Dempsey took my journal. I called him Regina, and no, I still won't write his name because he just might be reading this.

Although nothing ever happened between Regina and me, I was beginning to form an unhealthy relationship with myself. I blamed my hands for not being pretty enough for Regina to notice me. *If I only had ten fingers, then he'd like me,* I told myself. I began to believe what those few thought of me that I was some helpless disabled girl. I wanted to look normal like everyone else so bad just to stop all the staring and the judging. I was convinced that hiding my hands would somehow erase its deformed condition and stop all the curious looks. I continued to be in denial and hid my hands, but as I hid my hands I was slowly losing myself. I began to grow more and more dissonant in my life, clouding my judgment, blinding me from seeing my true self as I refused a very important part of myself: my hands.

I became paranoid and felt like everyone was sneaking stares at my hands. As my insecurities grew, I looked for any opportunities that would prove I was the strong, confident person I thought myself to be. So, in eighth grade I decided to run for student government. My school district had students from grades seven through nine attend together in junior high, and then we would transfer to high school for sophomore, junior, and senior years. Student body officers at my junior high were freshman. I wanted to run for office and learned that my cousin Suli wanted to run for the same position: Student Body President. I wanted both of us to be in office together, so I compromised and said I'd run for another position. But secretly, I was glad because I didn't know if I was ready for the attention I was going to get if I won as president.

There was an informational meeting for all interested candidates who wanted to run for office. Suli, Kerissa (the same friend from elementary school), and I attended the meeting. Suli signed up for the president position, I opted for the secretary position, and Kerissa chose Historian. We started working on meeting the requirements to run for office and was sad when Suli dropped out. Kerissa and I continued on with our campaigns and made it through to the final elections and won. Even though I was excited to win, I was really nervous and anxious because I knew I was going to be in the spotlight often.

Being a student body officer my freshman year kept me afloat. My insecurities grew worse and were getting the best of me. I started suffering from depression. I remember during my first meeting with my fellow student body officers, our advisor asked me to take the minutes since I was the secretary. I honestly didn't know what she meant and she could tell I didn't understand what she meant. She then explained what it meant and then I started taking the minutes. Feeling like a failure, I asked to go to the bathroom and started crying the moment I got there. I didn't want to go back to the meeting. I didn't even know what I was doing.

On many occasions, I would break down and cry and I didn't even know why. Sometimes I would cry for no reason and because I thought that was stupid I cried even more. I was not happy with myself and especially not happy with how I looked. I started comparing myself to my best friend Eme. Eme is a beautiful girl with a pretty face, and because she was beautiful on the inside, it just made her even more beautiful on the outside. I always admired that about her, and started to feel envious of her. People wanted to be around her. I was not surprised, but I was surprised with the negative feelings I started feeling towards her. I didn't understand why I felt that when she did nothing to me but be herself. She was always a great friend and always made sure to include me. But I began to notice the way people would look at her, particularly from boys, and compared that to the way people looked at me. I was falling into a very dark place emotionally.

I became defensive and felt like everyone was judging and belittling me. People would offer to help me, but I would feel so furious inside. *What? You don't think I can do it?* And I would quickly snap back a reply, "Oh, no! I don't need your help!" I started having a hard time trusting others and their intentions. I even lost trust in my closest friends and would question their loyalty, testing them if they really were my friend or just feeling sorry for me. I was putting my insecurities on them and it was affecting our relationship. I began to experience what is called cognitive dissonance, which is "the state of having inconsistent thoughts, beliefs, or attitudes, especially as relating to behavioral decisions and attitude change."[2]

Most of these people genuinely wanted to help me, but I was convinced everyone felt sorry for me and was looking down on me. I knew changing my hands was not an option. In order to protect myself, I decided the next best thing was to try my best to ignore its existence by hiding it. I was convinced that if the stares would stop, my problems would go away. I learned my freshman year a valuable lesson. That lesson was if you ever have a friend who can sit by you and wait, listen, and wait some more for you to finish crying and still want to be around you after that, then consider them a true friend. Eme and Mele were both that kind of friend. Kerissa was that kind of friend.

Kerissa and I met when we were in first grade. We were in the same class and instantly became friends. She was always supportive of me and my crazy ideas and even helped me with my sixth-grade recess concert. It was fun being a student body officer with her during our freshman year together especially since she was going to go to a different high school the following year.

One particular day, I was feeling extremely down on myself. We had our student government class right before lunch. As the bell rang for us to go to lunch, I stayed seated acting as if I was finishing up some work. As everyone filed out of the room, staring down at the clipboard on my desk, my eyes started filling up with tears. I tried my best to keep those tears inside my eyes just until everyone left the room, but they slowly started dripping down my face. Fidgeting with a binder clip, I silently cried hoping no one would walk through the door of the classroom. I soon heard footsteps approach the doorway.

"Leslie, are you going to eat?" It was Kerissa's voice.

I couldn't respond and continued to look down at my desk.

She then asked, "Leslie, are you okay?"

With my head down not responding to either question, she walked up to my desk, put her hand on my shoulder, and asked again, "Are you okay, Leslie?"

I couldn't hold it in any longer and started to sob. I didn't know how to respond, because, honestly, I didn't know if I was okay. I was having a hard time dealing with the emotions I felt, and I didn't know why I was always crying. These emotions I felt were too much for me to handle and process, and I felt lost and confused most of the time. As Kerissa sat beside me, I sobbed even more because I felt undeserving of her attention, and still she sat with me, silently, patting my shoulder. I eventually was able to stop crying and was able to speak.

"Sorry, Kerissa," I said. "I feel better now. Thank you."

She didn't say much to me that whole time, but her being there with me was all I needed to get through that crying spell. She sacrificed her lunch time to sit there and be with me, and I will never forget it.

Despite having frequent crying spells my freshman year, I tried my best to be happy, always laughing and smiling, whenever I was around my peers. Only my best and closest friends knew of my internal struggle and helped me through my crying spells. Being a student body officer that year allowed me many opportunities to develop my talents and learn new leadership skills. I was able to foster new relationships with others I wouldn't otherwise have met. But if there is one thing that was hard for me from the whole experience, it was facing my fears.

Toward the end of the school year, the student government from a neighboring junior high invited our student government to their school. They specifically invited us to attend their school dance and we excitedly agreed to go. When we arrived to their school, we were greeted by their student body president. He gave us a mini tour of their school, and light refreshments before attending their school dance. It was eye opening attending a different school and seeing how things were run there. The biggest difference with our schools were school uniforms. We weren't required to wear uniforms like they were.

Entering the school dance, we immediately stood out like a sore thumb. Thankfully there was quite a few of us in our group that I was able to linger towards the back of our group. As we enjoyed the music and dancing, their student body president asked if we could participate in a dancing activity they were going to start in a few minutes. We all agreed to help and waited for him to start the activity.

As he introduced us to their student body, he invited our student body and class presidents to the dance floor and paired them up with their student body officers. They were to slow dance with each other and then split to find new dance partners, continually doing this until everyone was dancing on the dance floor. As they started, I stood there watching, dreading my turn. Several changes had occurred when Mycal, my singing friend and president of his class, noticed I was still standing and watching. He came and got me to dance with him, and I reluctantly followed. As I danced with him, I was trying so hard to hide my anxiety. The next round I had to find someone to dance with and everyone I knew was already on the dance floor. I was looking around trying to figure out who I was going to ask and came to a brutal realization that I had no choice but to choose someone I didn't know.

Dreading the next split, I gave myself a pep talk and encouraged myself to find someone to dance with. I thought it no big deal. I'll ask someone to dance, and we'll dance, and I'll enjoy meeting new people the rest of our time here. It was now time to split. Mycal wished me luck, and I was off to find someone. I thought maybe I should find a Poly boy. I don't think they'd refuse me if I asked. But realizing how quick these changes occurred, I didn't want to be the last one to find a partner and look pathetic, so I went to the nearest boy I saw.

Luckily there was a group of boys near me. As I walked toward the nearest boy, I asked him to dance. He took a step back with a look of surprise and fear on his face. I was taken aback and thought, *Oh, maybe he's shy and doesn't like dancing.* So, I tried a second time taking another step toward his friend next to him. As I asked him to dance, he also took a step back and was shaking his head. By this time, I was feeling very uncomfortable and regretted approaching this group of boys. The funny thing is I still had an ounce of pride in me and attempted a third time. As I took another step toward the rest of their crew, they all stepped away from me as if I had a contagious disease. I could no longer hold back my tears nor bear the humiliation any longer.

I ran out of the gym and found a secluded dark hallway. I fell to the ground crying, no, sobbing so hard I had a hard time breathing. I was feeling sorry for myself as my thoughts were going crazy trying to make sense of what just happened:

This is what I was trying to avoid. This is why I try to hide my hands. I don't want people to be scared of me. I'm not a freak, I promise. Why can't they see me, the real me? I'm so much more than this body. I wish they would just give me a chance and get to know me, but they won't because of my stupid hands. I hate my hands. Why did I have to be born this way? Why couldn't I have normal hands? Did I do something bad to deserve this?

Feeling a mountain of emotions hit me all at once, I had no choice but to surrender and embrace it. Five minutes later, my friends found me. They did their best to comfort me. I don't even remember the words they said to me, but I do remember them sitting around me for a while. They tried their best to cheer me up, but I felt confused with my emotions. I was grateful they were there with me saying all these nice things, but I was skeptical. *Do they really mean what they're saying? I* wondered. *Are they taking pity on me? They won't ever understand what I'm going through.*

I felt miserable, furious, and hurt. They sat and waited for me to get up from the ground, but I learned with my crying spells it was hard to stop once I started and this time was no exception. I was frustrated with those boys, but more so with myself for asking them. I cried even more. Their student body president came looking for us, and soon found everyone huddled around me. Inquiring about the situation, he felt sorry and apologized on behalf of his student body. I know he meant well. Everyone did. But all their words of encouragement went in one ear and out the other. I was now experiencing a new low I never thought I'd ever feel, and I was having difficulty processing these new feelings.

After that incident, my depression grew worse. I was hiding more to cry in secret. The bathroom was the place I would usually go to at school when I felt like crying. My friends started noticing how I kept myself distant from them, and seemed more sad than usual. At home, I became angry all the time and took it out on my family. I kept to myself in my room.

It got real when I started contemplating suicide. I started to believe that my existence was a waste of time. The fact that I was born with these hands must be proof that I was a mistake. I started to believe life for everyone would be better without me in it. I imagined the different ways I could kill myself and even grabbed a knife to cut myself. But as I held the knife looking at my hands, I felt the eyes of the picture of Jesus, that hung on my wall, staring at me, piercing my mind and my heart to drop the knife. And the crazy thing is I was not looking at the picture. So, I put the knife away, came back to my room, and sat in bed staring at the picture of Christ hanging on my wall.

I haven't really shared much about Christ and where He fits in to my story. I want to begin with that picture in my room. Ever since my parents let me have my own room, they hung a picture of Christ on the wall. This picture is the portrait picture of Christ wearing a red robe. It's entitled "Jesus The Christ," by Del Parson, and it's a common painting of him you can find in Latter-day Saint chapels around the world.

I have spent countless hours sitting, staring at His face, having conversations with Him. Have you ever noticed how His face changes? I couldn't believe it at first, but as I would stare at His picture, I swear sometimes He was smiling at me. Other times, He had a stern look about Him and almost seemed disappointed in me. I became intrigued about that and thought either I was actually seeing the truth of how He felt about me or maybe I had completely lost it and was hallucinating.

My freshman year was the year we moved to the palangi ward. One Sunday, my bishop asked me to give a talk in sacrament meeting in two weeks' time. I didn't want to do it, but because my dad taught me to say yes to any call or assignment we received from our church leaders, I said yes. He gave me the topic I had to speak on, and that was that. Fast forward to two weeks later, I walked into sacrament meeting in shock as I read the program and saw my name on it as the youth speaker. I straightaway went and told the bishop that I could not speak that day. I had totally forgotten about it. The bishop was persistent and asked if I could just bear my testimony instead, so I reluctantly said yes.

I didn't want to sit up on the stand in front of the congregation, so I stood in the hallway outside of the chapel trying to figure out what I was going to say. I was giving myself a hard time for forgetting. I couldn't believe I forgot, and I'm usually good with remembering these kinds of things. As I waited for them to announce my name, I began to pray for inspiration. *What am I going to say?* But as I prayed, I could only think of how big of a hypocrite I was to be there in church. *I'm supposed to go up there and share my testimony when deep down inside I don't even know if I have one.*

I heard my name and was grateful I was first as the youth speaker. Walking into the chapel, I dreaded each step I took towards the pulpit. I don't remember exactly word for word what I said, but I do remember some key things that happened in that five-minute testimony that I gave. I first admitted to the ward that I had forgotten about speaking that day and then it happened. I wasn't planning on it, but I basically shared my internal struggles of self-worth, depression, and suicide. I cried as I expressed my desire to know why I had to be born this way. I didn't understand it, and was having a really hard time accepting my hands. Finishing up, I left my struggles out in the open and quickly bore my memorized Primary testimony. As I stood there looking out to the congregation, I just remember the concerned looks the people had on their faces. At that point, I didn't care what others thought about me, and I was glad I was finally done speaking.

This experience was the first time I ever said it—my struggles—out loud in the open. I had never done that before, not even with any of my close friends. My friends knew I was struggling every time I was being a crybaby, but I never opened up with them about why. They had a hunch about it, but they never pressured me to tell them. And of all places I would share it with, it had to be in church. I wasn't expecting that, but I'm glad it was in church.

Hearing myself say these things out loud confirmed what I was trying so hard to deny inside. I didn't want to admit that I had low self-esteem and that I was suffering from depression. I was trying all that time to prove that I was strong and confident in who I am as a person. After my testimony, I remember the bishop getting up and bearing his. He basically bore his testimony to me of self-worth in front of the whole ward. I felt a pinch of warmth in my heart.

That year, I was conflicted with who I was trying to be by denying who I really was as a person. I was confused. I was so focused on the exterior and on what other people thought of me that I lost sight of my worth as a human being and lost sight of God's infinite love for me. I looked to the world to define me when I should've been looking to God. And in the process, the dissonance grew irritatingly louder. It would take a few years for the Lord to help me resolve this dissonance I had in my life, but in the process of resolving the pain and sorrow from this conflict, I can honestly say the peace and joy I felt was much sweeter than I could've ever imagined it to be.

Notes

1. Google Dictionary, s.v. "dissonance," https://www.google.com.
2. Google Dictionary, s.v. "cognitive dissonance," https://www.google.com.

CHAPTER 6

Don't Diminish Me!

When I write songs, I tend to gravitate toward the darker, melancholy sounds by using minor notes and chords. I usually have minor chords in almost every stanza because of the depth of emotion I want to express in a song. Diminished chords are what I consider a super minor chord because of its unstable sound. If you sit in it too long, it'll make you feel uncomfortable and want to move. The word "diminish" itself means to become less. I don't know of anyone in this world who wants to become less in value, talent, knowledge, status, or beauty. It's natural for us to want more, to become more, and desire to improve. Starting high school was just that. I wanted to be more confident in myself, more attractive, and more popular. I wanted to be better than I was the year before.

Freshman year had been hard. I had a lot of fun with my friends. I sang and performed a lot. I made some great memories that year, and not-so-great memories I wish I could forget. I cried a lot in secret, and did my best to hide the fact that I was unhappy inside. Graduating from junior high school was a great day, and I was ready to be in high school. I was excited to be in a new place, meet new people, make some new friends, and especially get my driver's license.

My new school was less than a minute's drive from my junior high school, so that made the drive easier for my parents with drop-offs to and pick-ups from school. The night before the first day of high school, I made the decision that this year was going to be different from the last. I didn't want to be a crybaby anymore. I was sick of feeling sorry for myself. I was sick of appearing weak and helpless. This new school meant a fresh start and a new beginning. I was determined that this school year I was going to live it up.

My first day of school happened so fast. It was all a blur. The hallways were busier than what I was used to. The school campus was definitely bigger and student enrollment was larger. I must have gotten lost trying to find my classes several times that day. It was nice seeing familiar faces in the halls. It was even better seeing many new faces who could be potential friends and crushes. My dad didn't allow us to date until we finished school, so I knew I couldn't have any boyfriends, but I could admire people. It was just nice being in a new place. I wanted to fit in. I wanted to belong, but "where" was the question.

I identified myself with any singers since I loved to sing, the Polynesian people because I was Tongan, and with any members of the Church. Growing up in Utah, you take advantage of the accessibility of the Church, or at least I did. I didn't have to experience early morning seminary and had the option to take seminary during school as part of my class schedule. I was a bit shocked when I learned that not many places did that. I didn't have to travel hours to the nearest chapel or temple since they were found in every neighborhood. I didn't have to explain myself to anyone since the majority of my classmates were either Latter-day Saints or Christian.

Most of the Polynesian kids hung out with each other, and most of the time, our gathering place was the library. It became a refuge for me because it was the one place we had to be quiet, and that can be hard for Polynesians. I can't count how many times the librarian, Ms. Pray, would ask the Polys to be quiet, and we'd either listen or leave the library. The librarians became my favorite teachers, and they weren't even my actual teachers. But I could count on their door always being open. I could always go there for help with my homework. They did their best to assist me and always knew the best books that could help me.

The one thing I felt confident in was singing. I always felt good about myself when I'd sing, and I would use singing to make friends. If someone was jamming out on the guitar or ukulele in the halls, I'd stop to listen to them and enjoy the music. Sometimes they'd invite me to sing with them and that was always fun. The one habit I have with singing is I like to include those around me, and anyone who has been around me knows I'll ask you to sing a song. Music is a great way to connect with those around you. There's a powerful influence music brings to all participants, and it's become my hope by inviting others to join in the music that they'll feel what I feel. But I also ask people to join in so they don't feel left out either. I knew that feeling all too well; to be overlooked, to be judged as incapable, to not be given a chance.

There was one group I didn't identify myself with. I did not identify myself as disabled. I refused to. It just didn't make sense to me. How could I consider myself disabled when I was clearly able to do most things that everyone else can do? I wasn't dependent on others to help me do simple things. Yes, I did things differently, but I was doing it myself.

During my sophomore year, I continued to hide my hands just as I did in ninth grade. And there were times where I cried, but it was way less than the year before. Instead, I became angry. I was angry because I felt diminished. People were still staring at me the way they did. I assumed people thought me incapable of doing normal everyday things because they always offered to help me. I was angry that I was looked down upon and not given a chance to show myself. Even though I was angry with the world around me, I was more so angry with myself. I became angry that I was born this way and didn't understand why God would do this to me.

Despite my insecurities, I really liked socializing and making friends. My sophomore year I made lots of friends, but because I wanted to prove that I was just as normal as everyone else and that I was worth being a friend with, I got myself into trouble. The first semester of tenth grade was coming to a close, and we had to register for classes for the next semester. They had registration in the cafeteria. My friends and I went together in hopes that we'd sign up for the same classes.

As our class schedule started filling up, I still needed to sign up for an elective class. My friend Ema also needed to take an elective. We decided to look for a class that had room for the both of us. We had to quickly sign up for a class as registration was closing in five minutes. We saw a table that had the sign *drafting* on it, and saw the teacher had plenty of room on his list. We signed up for that class as an elective and had no clue what we were getting ourselves into.

The first day of class, Ema and I walked into the classroom, surprised that it was a workshop. We settled ourselves in the back corner table of the room. We both just giggled amongst ourselves in regret for not thoroughly inquiring about the class. We eagerly awaited the teacher's instructions and hoped the class was something we'd be interested in. As the teacher went through attendance, we looked around and realized we were the only girls in the room. *What the heck did we just sign up for?*

This class was basically an introduction into the world of architects, drafters, and engineers. We learned that we were going to draft floor plans for different buildings on paper and electronically on the computer. We had a big project at the end of the year to build a miniature of our floor plans we were going to draft throughout the semester. Ema and I started debating whether we should drop out of the class or stick with it. We decided to stay.

At the start we did good attending class, but we soon lost interest and just started skipping that class. As I skipped that class, it became easier for me to skip my other classes. We would go joy riding around the city and would find ourselves at 7-Eleven, Jamba Juice across the street, or at any of the fast food restaurants nearby. Sometimes we'd go visit our friends at other schools. My high school was by a park, and we spent a lot of time hanging out at the pavilion just talking and laughing.

I started cussing just to try it out. It was weird at first, but I was determined to be cool so I thought. I started trying to fit in as many cuss words I could in a sentence. It was ridiculous. I'm still in disbelief as I'm writing this. Walking out of school one day, I remember distinctly feeling drained as I generously threw out a, "F-this" and "F-that." I started to feel something I never noticed before, and I was trying to figure out what that feeling was. I recognized an emptiness that continued to grow within me with every bad word and deed. I later learned that emptiness was the loss of God's Spirit in my life. I was depriving my spirit from needed nourishment from God's Spirit. It's funny how I tried so hard to increase my popularity and in the process diminished the influence of the Holy Ghost in my life.

That last semester of my sophomore year was spent just playing around trying to fit in. When I got my final grades for that semester, I had failed several of my classes, including drafting, and had the lowest grades I ever had. I knew my parents were going to kill me when they saw my grades. I tried my hardest to keep my report card from them as long as I could, but it didn't help when my brothers showed their report card to my parents and they asked to see mine. I was so mad at them especially since they had better grades than me. My dad saw my report card and immediately started scratching his head, and when he scratches his head, my siblings and I know he's upset.

I moved to the furthest part of the room from my parents in hopes of dodging any smacks upside my head. My mom was really good at that, especially when I least expected it. I was waiting for them to blow up, but surprisingly they didn't. Instead, they started asking me questions about my report card. I had to take classes that summer to make up for the credits I lost. I was not happy about that, but I was grateful that my parents took me to classes instead of making me walk to school. Utah's summer heat is unforgiving and no one wants to be walking in that dry heat, or at least I didn't want to.

That year, I tried to prove myself to my friends, and in the end I had to pay the price and face the consequences of my bad choices. As I focused on proving myself to my friends, I lost a sense of myself in the process. That year was also difficult for me because I lost my last living grandparent, Grandma Fatai. When she passed away, I didn't realize the impact her passing would have on me. My parents had told me the news of her passing when they picked me up from school one day, and I couldn't believe them. I'll never forget how numb I felt. I had so many questions and asked if I could go to her funeral in Tonga. I figured it would make sense for me to go since I was her namesake, but my parents said no. We didn't have the money.

When I got to my room, I just sat on my bed trying to process what had just happened and what that meant to me. I could overhear my parents talk about making the trip to Tonga for her funeral. I wanted to go badly and felt immensely sad. I cried reflecting on the memories I had with her. Although they were not many, the experiences I did have with her left a deep impression on me, and I have always been fond of her. Now that she passed away, I felt the weight of her name. She left some big shoes to fill. I felt like I needed to prove myself to my family and to all those who knew her that giving her name to me was not in vain. She had set the bar high, and I will admit I was a bit discouraged. I was nowhere near like her. I felt I had the singing part down, but everything else she was I needed to work on. I wasn't the great big sister I should be. I avoided working hard, and my faith was faltering. I didn't know what I believed in. I just went through the motions with church saying what I needed to say, doing what I needed to do, and being what I needed to be.

With the pressures of fitting in with my peers and living up to my family's expectations, I didn't know myself anymore. I was living two different lives, and I wasn't happy with where my life was headed. I didn't like how I looked and wished badly to change my hands. My mom always knew I was struggling, but she didn't know what to say to me. She did her best to uplift me whenever I was feeling down on myself, but even that wasn't enough. I was still convinced that if my hands were normal like everyone else, all my problems would be gone and I would be happy. What I didn't realize was I was diminishing myself by using my insecurities to fuel a false reality I had created for myself. Focusing on my insecurities drove me to be something that I truly wasn't, thus, losing and diminishing important parts of my true self as a child of God.

One evening, my family was eating out at a restaurant. While I was in the bathroom, a nice older woman approached my parents and asked about me and my hands. She was a nurse and spoke with my parents about possible surgeries I could have on my hands to make life easier for me. She left her information with them, and my parents were interested. They later told me about it when I returned back to our table that the lady had spoken of a toe-to-hand implantation surgery where they'd take my toe and implant it on my hand as my thumb. I laughed and thought it was the funniest thing I ever heard.

I honestly didn't know what to think. If I use my toe as a thumb, is it no longer called a toe even if it still looks and smells like one? I couldn't get over the thought that my hand might possibly smell like feet, and I wasn't ready to smell feet all the time, especially during meal time. Do you realize how often your hands touch your face? And how often you might lick your fingers? And I understood there were people who didn't have arms and hands and had to use their feet for everything, but I had been using *these* hands my whole life, and I wasn't sure if I was ready to have my toe touch my face or my food for that matter.

Well, my mom decided to look up a specialist and made an appointment. On our way to the appointment, I was feeling a bit nervous and scared. All this time I wished and hoped that I could change my hands, and here I was one step closer to seeing that become a reality. When we arrived, we took some x-rays of my hands and waited to see the doctor. When we met with the doctor, I started having mixed feelings about the whole thing. As he asked me simple questions about my hands, I started to feel ashamed that I was even there. Don't get me wrong, I felt excited at the possibility of fixing my hair up in a ponytail for the first time in my life, but I was starting to wonder if this surgery would really solve my problems and make me feel happy about myself. I felt unsure about the surgery so the doctor advised us to think about it and contact him when we felt ready to go through with it.

On our way home, I was stuck in my thoughts thinking of my hands and imagined how it would look like post-surgery. Having toes as fingers was not what I pictured, so we backed out of that and never looked back at any kind of surgery again. I wanted to make my hands better. Having only five fingers just wasn't enough, and since surgery was no longer an option for me, I was left to daydream about having normal hands and how amazing of a person I could've been.

I actually found myself daydreaming a lot. One summer, my stake had youth camp at a ranch. Each ward was assigned cabins. The boys had their side of the cabin, and the girls were on the other side. Every day, we had fun activities planned out throughout the ranch. Whenever we had downtime, I'd go walk around with snacks in hand to explore the ranch and see what everyone else was doing. I usually found myself sitting in the bleachers watching kids play basketball or volleyball.

During some downtime one day, I watched my ward's youth playing volleyball with some other youth in the stake. As I sat there eating some licorice, I imagined myself playing volleyball with them. Bumping the ball wouldn't hurt me. I'd set the ball flawlessly, and it would go where I wanted it to go. And when I'd spike, I'd spike the heck out of the ball. Man! No one would want to mess with me. I'd be the coolest person on the court if everyone could see what I saw in my mind.

That was a habit I had with any sport. I'd daydream of basketball. There I'd be dribbling down the court so fast, breaking ankles, and dunking the ball like crazy. Softball. Even football. But don't get me started on dancing. Ain't no one ever seen these moves before. But as I lived in my mind with the what-ifs and what could be, I was always reminded of my reality and felt worthless again.

During youth camp, we had the opportunity to go horseback riding. Each ward had a designated time to go with their youth, and soon it was our time to go. I must admit, I was a little anxious, but was more excited to go since this was my first time going horseback riding. I checked my shoulder bag and made sure I had snacks in it. I grabbed my CD player and headed to our meeting place with some of the girls I was rooming with.

As we arrived, everyone was waiting, excitedly sharing any previous horseback-riding experiences. I was glad I wasn't the only one experiencing this for the first time. Our guides greeted us and led us to the horses. They instructed us to find a horse and use the provided mounting blocks to mount our horses. As I approached my horse, I didn't realize how big these horses were. I tried not to be scared but I was scared. You know how they say horses are sensitive animals and can sense your emotions? Well, I knew my horse sensed my fear. As I got on him, he was a bit unsettled, moving around more than usual. That didn't help me one bit because I knew if I was going to survive this ride, I needed to get a grip of myself and remain calm in order to make it to the end. I was praying he wouldn't buck me off.

Once everyone was on their horses and ready to go, our guides started us on the path. I was towards the back of the line. Watching everyone start to move had me holding my breath as I waited for my horse to move. When he moved, all the muscles of my body tightened as I held tight to the reins and saddle horn. *Wow!* I was amazed at the movements of the horse. I slowly started to relax when I realized how slow the horse was moving. It was walking a very slow pace which allowed me to take in the beauty of the mountainside we were walking through.

My fear was soon replaced with confidence and I slowly grew irritated at the speed we were going. I started imagining how fun it would be if I could go fast with my horse like in the movies. I was getting bored and hoped to see some kind of action. You know the saying, "be careful what you wish for because it might just come true"? Well, that phrase punched me in the face the minutes that followed.

Looking into my bag, I didn't want to eat any of the snacks I brought so I grabbed my earphones and started listening to music on my CD player. I was very inconsiderate of everyone around me and started singing along with my music, and loudly at that. I noticed we were approaching the end of the trail and so I turned off my music and put my earphones away. The majority of the trail we rode through was narrow, but we were approaching a beautiful open field. It was at that moment my horse raced out of the line and galloped towards the open field, bucking me off his back where I landed on a large rock hidden in the wild flowers. I felt a sharp pain move from my butt to my back. I tried to get up, but the pain was too much to handle. I couldn't move. I laid there in disbelief that this happened. Everything I didn't want to happen happened and I was so embarrassed. I didn't know what hurt more, my body or my pride.

I was soon greeted by my youth leaders as they helped me up and got me back to our cabin. Everyone was so attentive and did their best to care for me. Lying in bed was very uncomfortable. It was hard trying to find a comfortable position, but I was able to finally lay on the opposite side of where I landed on the rock. The girls sat and kept me company as we talked about the horseback ride and everything we did that day. As they left for dinner, I laid in my bed reflecting on what just happened. *Why did that horse do that to me? The other horses didn't buck their riders. Was it my singing? Is my voice that bad? Did the horse know what I was thinking?* I soon fell asleep.

I learned more about horses and their keen sense of human emotion. I was amazed to learn how in tune these animals are with their rider. This horse sensed how unstable I was in my heart and soul. And even though I was trying my hardest to mask the internal struggle I dealt with daily from everyone around me, this horse knew. And he knew I needed a wake-up call.

The next day, I painfully felt everything completely. My body felt paralyzed and broken. I tried getting out of bed, but I couldn't move. I laid in bed for at least an hour until finally I got the strength to pull myself up. Holding on to the bars of the upper bunk bed, I did my best to move myself in sitting position. It was the last day of camp, and I was going home in a matter of hours. I was glad too. When you're in pain or feeling sick, nothing makes you feel better than being home, having your mom beside you caring for you. I couldn't wait to get home.

Before leaving camp, my bishop and some other priesthood holders came to our cabin to give me a priesthood blessing of healing. We all shared small talk, and then they called for me to come to the center of the room. As I got up, I tried my hardest to show no pain in my face with every step I took. *I'm strong*, I thought. *They need to see that I'm strong.*

As I finally made my way to the chair, the feeling of the room changed. There was an immense feeling of peace in the room. It felt so warm that even my pain was melting away. I could sit in this feeling forever. I felt love. Complete, unconditional love for me. I looked around the room that day. Each young woman I saw now as my sisters. My young women leaders had this motherly look on their faces. Every Sunday, they always expressed their love for me and the girls, but in this very moment I finally understood and felt it. They really meant it. They always did.

I don't remember exactly what my bishop said to me in that blessing, but I do remember how I felt before, during, and after the blessing. The blessing was powerful and the Spirit slowly melted all my doubts and fears away. I no longer felt diminished, but uplifted, strengthened, and completely loved for who I was even in my brokenness. The Lord said "the worth of souls is great in the sight of God" (D&C 18:10), and I got a glimpse of my worth as I felt an increase of God's love in that very moment. If what I was feeling was real, I knew I needed to feel more of it in my life to replace the negative feelings I was struggling with from low self-esteem and depression.

Chapter 7

Show Yourself

You're probably wondering, well, how did I come to accept my hands? I can tell you it didn't happen overnight. It took me a while to come to terms with my hands. I was fighting so hard to deny their existence, and in the process, I lost myself. You don't realize how important your hands are or any other part of your body is until you're unable to do everyday things that you usually take for granted. But I didn't have that experience. I've only known these hands. These hands were my hands, and I never thought twice about it until I started focusing on what everyone else had that I didn't— two normal, five-fingered hands.

Losing my sense of self was like digging a hole. With every experience I had comparing myself to others, I dug the hole a little deeper. Every comment and stare brought me lower into that hole. I couldn't see the light out of the hole, and became stuck in complete darkness. I spent a lot of time in that hole that when I began to see flickers of light coming in from outside the hole, I was scared and even felt ashamed to come out. I had grown so comfortable in the darkness that I bathed in it. What I failed to see was the many hands reaching down trying to pull me out. They knew I was down there and did their best to reach me. It wasn't until someone came into my dark hole, and helped me come out and face the blinding light.

You're probably wondering who that someone was. If you haven't figured it out by now, that someone was my dad. A parent just knows when something is going on with their child. Although I never told them, my parents recognized something was going on with me. They just had a hunch. They saw how I was always upset and angry at home. They noticed my behavior regarding my hands. For me as a parent now, I can understand how cautious they were in approaching me. I was like a walking time bomb about to blow up.

During FHE one night, my dad was making his rounds with each member of the family. This was the time that he'd check in with each of us. He'd ask each of us what we learned in church, how we are doing, any plans we had the coming week, and to give us counsel if needed. I wasn't too fond of the counseling part. He'd usually counsel us if we had a problem that week, or if he saw we needed to work on something to be better.

When it was my turn, my dad asked his probing questions, and I did my best to poker face it and act like everything was great. I kept my answers short and sweet, and I hoped he'd be satisfied with them and move on. I remember there was silence, and I thought, *Yes! My turn is done.* I had zoned out by this time thinking my turn was done. Realizing he was still speaking to me, I heard, "Fatai, you're a daughter of God. Heavenly Father loves you." I knew what he was talking about. He wanted me to remember who I was. I took it lightly and brushed it off. *I'm doing okay*, I thought. *He has to say those kinds of things to me because he's my dad. That's his job.* So, I continued hiding my hands and took my frustration out on my family.

One day, my dad felt prompted to take me with him to pick up something from his work office. We had arrived to his work office. I waited in the van as he did what he needed to do inside. In less than ten minutes we were back on the road heading home. My dad made small talk with me asking me how I was doing in school and about my friends, and then he spoke frankly with me. "Fatai," he said, "I know why you hide your hands." I was taken back by his speech. I didn't expect him to say those words to me. He continued to speak, "You need to show yourself. Show yourself and they will love you." I was lost in my thoughts trying to process his words. *Show myself. What does he mean? Show my hands?* I was trying to understand how people could love me if they saw my hands.

After that car ride, I thought a lot about my dad's words. I've always trusted my dad and started considering his counsel, but I had a hard time trying to visualize how to show myself. All this time I hid my hands because I felt people were scared or they were looking down on me. My problem was I believed them. If they felt sorry for me, I would feel sorry for myself. If they didn't like my hands, I didn't like my hands. And the crazy part is, all these people were people I didn't know. Those closest to me never showed fear or disgust for my hands. It was the opposite. I came to a brutal realization that I cared so much about everyone's opinion but my own. And in the process, I lost myself.

I had to learn how to love myself again. Not the fake, pretend I'm amazing kind of self-love, but true genuine love of self. So, I started wearing short-sleeved shirts. At first, I felt so naked having my hands uncovered. I'd walk around with my teeth clenched trying hard to avoid eye contact with anyone. I didn't want anyone to see how vulnerable I felt.

I realized I had a bad habit of unconsciously hiding my hands. I'd find myself hiding my hands behind my back or in my pockets. I wanted to stop this bad habit, so I consciously made the effort to move my hands from my back to my sides and out of my pockets. I admit it was mentally draining to train my brain to think differently and to train my body to react differently. If I felt I was being judged, I'd quickly move to hide my hands without even thinking. I started catching myself react that way and would purposely move my hands to be seen. I did this, not to show everyone that I was no longer ashamed, but to show myself that I don't need to hide anymore, that I was worth being seen for me in all my imperfections.

I started noticing more looks of approval from my friends and peers. I wasn't looking for their approval, but I felt acknowledged. I was beginning to feel good about myself. I was feeling at peace with my life. As I worked on changing some of my bad habits, I sought opportunities that would get me out of my comfort zone. Each time I stepped out of my comfort zone I discovered something new about myself.

Toward the end of my junior year, I decided to run for student government again. This would be the second time I'd run, and I wasn't as scared as I was the first time around. With this newfound confidence in myself, I was ready to run for Student Body Office. I ran for vice-president and won my office seat. I was blown away by the support I received from my peers. Had they always liked me? Before, I was so focused on the negatives and totally missed all the smiles and kind words people shared with me every day. My dad was right. "Show yourself and they will love you."

Another experience I had was teaching choir in high school. Mr. Sparks was the choir teacher, and he decided to start a multicultural choir my junior year. The majority of the students taking the class were of Polynesian descent, so we called the choir Poly Choir. Mr. Sparks invited guest teachers to teach the choir cultural songs. Most of those guest teachers were parents of a student. My dad was able to come and guest-teach the choir. He taught the choir some Polynesian songs throughout the year, and we were able to showcase those songs in our concerts.

I had the opportunity to guest teach the multicultural choir as well. The only experience I had prior to that was teaching my cousins at family reunions and Eme and Mele. The Poly Choir had about forty students, and teaching a group of people that large was definitely a new experience for me.

Conducting was definitely out of my comfort zone. Whenever I sing in a choir setting, I watch the conductor's hands like a hawk. I've always been intrigued with the story those hands tell. And if you've never been in choir before, a conductor's hands have the greatest impact on a song. My first day of teaching, I was intimidated because I didn't know how the class would interpret my hand movements. I had practiced at home in front of the mirror, and I'll admit I felt silly as I tried to figure out which hand movements would be obvious for go and stop. As I started teaching, I couldn't help but notice the blank stares I got from students staring at my hands. I understood they'd never seen my hands, or any hands like my hands, move that way. They were trying to make sense of what my hand movements meant. I brushed the negative thoughts aside and focused on the music.

I depended on the piano to help me teach. I would sometimes lead the choir from behind the piano just like Ms. Straussberg had. So many times I wouldn't know how to sing certain parts, and I'd turn to the piano keys to teach it for me. I depended on those keys a lot. The piano brought my ideas to life. I have grown to love the piano for its reflection of my capabilities and not my disability. That was the greatest lesson the piano taught me.

You can imagine the nerves I experienced my first school concert. I was sweating bullets waiting for my turn to conduct the choir in front of the large audience that night. It was comforting to know I didn't have to face the audience to conduct, but even to this day, having to be up in front of a large group is a feeling I don't think I'll ever get used to. Every time I perform, I experience a wide spectrum of emotion. I'm nervous, excited, super scared, or antsy. But when the moment comes for me to perform, I am in the moment and forget everything but the music. I am grateful I was able to teach what I wanted to teach, and especially grateful the choir sang my songs beautifully. If there's anything I learned from this experience is you'll never know what you're capable of until you get of your comfort zone.

During the same time I was teaching the Poly Choir, I was also pursuing a solo career in music. I signed a recording contract with a small record label out in Orlando, Florida. My dad is employed for Delta Airlines and his work benefits has allowed my family to fly free wherever Delta flew. So, I made frequent visits to Florida every weekend and stayed with my aunty Vake. She and her family were living in Orlando at the time, and the record deal was only made possible because of them. My dad would've never let me go if we didn't have family he could trust to care for me.

I started writing more songs to take to Orlando. We spent a lot of time, many long nights, fine-tuning my songs and recording them in the studio. I met some very talented artists who were also signed to the label. Each artist had a different sound which made the label unique. We had a few shows coming up and we needed to put my portfolio together. I had my very first photoshoot experience. Fortunately, Aunty Vake was there to help me with wardrobe because I had no clue about fashion. Getting ready for the shoot was my favorite part of that experience. There's something about getting your hair and makeup done that does something to your confidence. I felt like a new person.

We met at some old train tracks to start the shoot. I felt uncomfortable being in front of the camera. As the shoot progressed I started to feel at ease. After we had enough shots at the train tracks, we had to leave to a new location. Keep in mind, I didn't really know what was going on. I was told to be here, go there, do that, smile like this, so I did all of that. My aunty was on the phone when I overheard her say, "It's red?" I was curious to know what was red.

As we got to our new location, my aunty had me change into a new outfit. I grew curious to know what was this red thing my aunty spoke of. After I changed, I could hear them in a nearby room. As I walked into the room, there on the stage was a bright red grand piano. It was the most beautiful piano I had ever seen. I walked up to the piano admiring its every curve. I tried to contain my excitement, but couldn't. I sat down and played its keys. I was mesmerized by its crisp sound. I swear I've played really good pianos before, but this piano was different. Maybe it was because it was red. Hypnotized, I didn't realize the photographer started taking a few shots of me playing. I was so ready to be done with this photo shoot. Lucky for me, the photographer let me play during the shoot. Those pictures turned out better than I thought it would. Nothing looked forced or rehearsed. It was evident I felt at home with the piano.

I had a few shows coming up. The biggest one I had to prepare for was a show my label was putting on for some big-time record labels. The venue was a nightclub called Key Club in West Hollywood, California. My label was showcasing each of their artists in hopes that these major record labels would be interested. I had my song list ready and spent a lot of time practicing in the studio and at home. I was excited for the experience, but really nervous because this was going to be my first time being in a nightclub.

The week of the showcase, I flew in to Los Angeles from home. My management picked me up and brought me to hang out with the other artists. For some of the artists, this was their first time in Los Angeles and it was a big deal for them. We went sightseeing around town and ended up at Venice Beach Boardwalk. Although it wasn't my first time there, it was refreshing for me to go with people who've never been. I couldn't help but notice the simple things I would've overlooked had they not been there.

Next day was the big day. We arrived early at the venue for sound check. As I entered the club, it was everything I imagined it to be: dark, mysterious, and the room felt a little stuffy. I was, however, surprised at the size of the room. It was smaller than what I expected. As I surveyed the room, I could only imagine the stories and secrets these walls could tell. Walking to take a look backstage, I saw a door signed by artists who performed on this very stage. Most of the names I saw on that door were rock bands. I only recognized the more popular rock bands like Van Halen and Guns N' Roses. There were a few hip-hop artists like Lil Kim and Warren G. I thought to myself as I scanned the stage, *They performed on this?*

As I looked out to where the crowd will be that night, I was beginning to feel the nerves and tried to suppress those feelings. I decided to explore more of the club to keep my mind occupied. I followed the other artists entering the side door of the stage. We had walked into what looked like a VIP lounge area. It was a pretty big room. The room was lined with neon lights all along the walls. In the back of the room was a hallway that led to smaller rooms. They designated those rooms as our dressing rooms. Walking through that whole area had me spooked.

Everything was dimly lit and I felt like some ghost was going to jump out at any moment. I tried not to be scared, but my nerves for the performance was already getting the best of me.

Sound check began and I sat watching the other artists perform. I felt my stomach in knots as I awaited my turn. These artists have been performing way longer than I have in these kinds of settings, and you could tell in their performance how comfortable they felt being on that stage. I usually sang in church or at school. I started to question myself why I decided to even do this. I began to doubt if I could even perform that night.

It was soon my turn for sound check. I felt numb with every step I took to the stage. I was trying hard to hide my discomfort from my face. I felt like I was going to vomit. They told me where to stand, and gave me the microphone to sing. As the track started, I began to sing. My nervousness affected my singing, and they stopped me midway to give me instructions. I had completely zoned out. I didn't hear a single word they said. I soon realized they had asked me a question and were looking at me intently for an answer. I didn't hear the question so I had no idea what to say. I was overwhelmed with the pressure and I began to cry.

The other artists were used to this. I wasn't. I was a newbie and I needed extra help, especially with where my confidence was at. Feeling like a complete utter failure, I wanted to run and hide. They softened their tone of voice and asked if I could continue with the rehearsal. I couldn't so they excused me to calm my nerves down.

A couple hours later, my parents arrived to the club. I was in my dressing room getting ready when my door opened and my parents greeted me. I felt relieved. *Finally! I can breathe,* I thought. Them being there was all I needed to keep me grounded in this foreign space. I was struggling to take in that kind of environment and the pressures that come with it. My management told my parents about sound check. My dad looked at me and asked, "Do you want a blessing?" I nodded yes and felt my eyes start to water. By this time, my hair and makeup were done. Everyone cleared the room except me and my parents. My dad then proceeded to give me a father's blessing of comfort.

Now, if you're not familiar with the Church of Jesus Christ, you may be wondering, how can my dad give me a blessing? Is he some kind of priest or rabbi? In my faith, we believe in the priesthood. The priesthood simply put is the power of God. Everyone, regardless of what kind of god you worship and believe in, has access to this power. The most common way is through prayer. The difference that our church has from others is we've been given authority to exercise priesthood power on behalf of the Lord. This authority was given as priesthood keys. They were given by the laying on of hands to Joseph Smith in the nineteenth century.

You'll hear members of the Church often talk about a restoration. The last time the priesthood keys were on the earth was during the time that Jesus and his twelve apostles had walked the earth. But as each one was martyred, we lost those keys. Thanks to the restoration of those priesthood keys through Joseph Smith, every worthy male is able to hold the priesthood power today. They are able to bless their family just as my father has done so throughout my life. The one who holds all priesthood keys today is the president of the Church of Jesus Christ of Latter-day Saints. Those priesthood keys are essential for the salvation and exaltation of man.

When people think of the priesthood, they immediately think of a man. They think that men *are* the priesthood. That notion is false. Although men are given the responsibility to hold the priesthood, everyone has access to its power. The priesthood is not defined by its holder, but by the faithfulness of its participants. I have always felt I could access the priesthood and it's been my security blanket, especially in times where I needed the Lord's help with my personal struggles. This is the power Joseph used to bring forth the Book of Mormon. And although the church has been heavily scrutinized for not letting women hold the priesthood like men do, I have never felt excluded. It's better to trust in the Lord's ways, for His ways are higher than our ways (see Isaiah 55:8–9).

My dad reminded me in the blessing of the purpose behind my talents and he blessed me to do my best. He reminded me of the Lord's revelation to Joseph Smith about talents. In that scripture, the Lord said, "to every man is given a gift by the Spirit of God. . . . And all these gifts come from God, for the benefit of the children of God" (D&C 46:11, 26). My father's blessing was exactly what I needed to hear, and I felt ready for my performance.

As I entered the VIP Lounge, the other artists were talking and waiting for the show to start. As I said my goodbyes to my parents, I was curious to see how many people were in the audience. I looked out and saw the room was full of people. I scanned the room to see any familiar faces, and found my family relatives enjoying themselves. I heard the host introduce the first act, and I knew I needed to get ready because I was next. The stage manager found me and asked me a few questions about my set since I didn't have sound check. He gave me some last instructions and wished me luck. I knew I was going to need it.

The other artists wished me luck and told me to be aware of the upper level. Our important guests were seated up there. Soon enough it was my turn to hit the stage, and I found myself on a brightly lit stage. I could not see any faces, but the silhouettes of people in the audience. That was a tender mercy.

As I started singing, it was exhilarating. The crowd's energy boosted my confidence. When I did my piano number, I could feel people staring at my hands. I felt a burning sensation in my hands. My fingertips started sweating profusely to the point that they started slipping on the keys. *Get yourself together, Fatai,* I thought as I tried to play each key.

My set was finally done. I managed to sing and play my songs, and I was relieved to finally get off the stage. I was enjoying the rest of the night watching the show when I was asked for an encore later that night. It's flattering to feel wanted, but I had enough of the stage for one night. I ended up singing another song, but I learned something about myself that day. I didn't want to be that kind of artist. I didn't like that kind of pressure, and I definitely didn't like performing in that type of environment. I had tasted enough of Hollywood to know for myself that it wasn't for me, even if it was a brief taste. I knew it would not make me happy and I had already made so much progress climbing out of the dark hole. I didn't want to do anything that would compromise the joy I was beginning to feel in my life being out in the light.

One last experience I want to share is from when I was fourteen years old. My family traveled to Tonga for a family reunion. We had arrived at the start of the Heilala Festival, which is an annual birthday celebration for the King of Tonga. This festival is highlighted by the Miss Heilala Beauty Pageant, a talent competition, and various shows and performances. That year, I participated in the talent competition. Winners would receive prize money and a chance to perform for the king.

This talent competition is the only kind of competition I've ever competed in, thanks to my uncle Hopoi. I never would've participated, but he signed me up for it because he knew I enjoyed singing. People have often asked me if I've ever tried out for *American Idol, The Voice,* or any other talent competitions. The truth is I never have, although I've heard a rumor that I did, which is amusing to me. The real reason is I was never enticed to audition because of the attention I would get if I were to—specifically the attention my hands would get. As a young teenager, I had a bad habit of comparing myself and struggling with low self-esteem and depression that I did not want to expose myself on that big of a stage.

Since my uncle signed me up, I was obedient and prepared for the talent competition. I won't lie. I was excited to sing, but really nervous. At the start of the competition, I sang the song "Beauty and the Beast." That song got me through each round to the final round. In the final round, I was able to sing my original song, "Shining Star," and dedicated that number to the Ofa Tui 'Amanaki (OTA) Centre for special needs kids in Tonga. This song won me the competition, but I'm not sharing this experience to brag that I won. It's what happened after that left a deep impression on my spirit and in my life.

After I was pronounced the winner, my dad told me, "Fatai, we are going to donate your prize money to the OTA." I thought I heard him wrong and replied, "What did you say?" He said again, "We will donate your prize money to the OTA" He gave me the serious look and I knew I couldn't argue with him. I was a little bitter about it, but I knew my dad had his reasons and obeyed. I not only won my age bracket, but the talent competition overall. I was named soloist of the year and had the opportunity to perform for the king. I never would've thought my own song would win me the competition. My family was proud. I was proud. Even my parents' villages were proud.

My dad had arranged a meeting with the OTA Education Centre, and a few days later, we were there to give our donation. The director of the center welcomed us warmly and brought us inside for a quick tour. He brought us into a room to meet their students. As I looked around the room at each child, I was deeply impressed by the spirit I felt in that room. I could only see a handful of children in the room, but the room felt full of people. It was as if each child had guardian angels surrounding them. I'll never forget how I felt being in that room with those precious spirits.

I enjoyed interacting with some of the kids. There was one kid who was funny and very talkative. I tried getting the attention of some kids, but they avoided eye contact with me and continued to play with their toys. My sister Vicelia and I performed some songs for the kids and we officially handed them our donation. I felt really selfish and regretted feeling bitter about donating my prize money. I knew our donation would help the facility and their work they were doing for these kids. I was grateful for the experience that day. Winning the prize money for them made it all worth it in the end.

I've learned from this experience and all the other experiences I've shared how important it is to give of yourself to find yourself. The Savior Himself even said, "For whosoever will save his life shall lose it: and whosoever will lose his life for my sake shall find it" (Matthew 16:25). That's been the main theme I've gotten from my dad's influence all throughout my life: to look for opportunities to serve those in need, giving of your time, your gifts, your talents, and your means, if possible. Even if it's not much, you have something to give. I have something to give. And as I show myself, I learn more of who I am, what I'm capable of doing while focusing on where and how my strengths can be a blessing to others.

CHAPTER 8

Grace Notes

G race notes usually don't play a major role in music. They're considered an afterthought only meant to embellish its main parts. Truthfully, I have a hard time playing grace notes on the piano because of their nature and my own lack of fingers. Grace notes come and go quickly, and if you don't pay attention, you'll miss it entirely. But why would I speak of grace notes if I struggle playing them? In our lives, we experience these grace notes. They add meaning to your life. These are the moments that come and go in our lives reminding us of our divine nature and our individual worth. It can come unexpectedly and in the most obvious ways. They are the tender mercies the Lord sends as a hug reassuring you that you can do hard things and that he loves you.

A grace note of mine was seminary. Seminary is a worldwide four-year religious educational program for youth ages fourteen to eighteen. The Church operates this program for the youth members, but it is open to youth of all faiths. Each year is focused on studying a different volume of scripture which includes the Old Testament, New Testament, Book of Mormon, and Doctrine and Covenants. I started going to seminary my freshman year. My seminary teacher, Brother Bawden, made class interesting and fun. My sophomore year, I had Brother

Christensen as my seminary teacher. I missed a lot of his class, along with every other class I was skipping, and had to make up my missed time in his class. But the seminary teacher I want to tell you about is Brother Beebe.

My junior year of high school I had Brother Beebe. He was known as the favorite seminary teacher. Any student who had him as a teacher only had good things to say about him, and that was a big deal. I was curious about him my sophomore year and was happy to find out he'd be my teacher my junior year. You know Fred Rogers from *Mister Rogers' Neighborhood*? Brother Beebe looked like the older version of Mr. Rogers. He had this friendly demeanor, and you always felt welcomed in his class. I even brought some of my nonmember friends to seminary with me and they felt the same way. My friends would invite me to skip my seminary class, but I didn't want to miss seminary, so instead I brought them with me. This was the first class I didn't want to miss, and it was because of Brother Beebe.

Any time I'd see him, he was always smiling. Even his resting face looked like he was smiling. He always seemed cheerful and happy to be there in seminary. I don't think I ever remember his classroom being empty. There was always someone in there. They would be studying doing homework. Others would be hanging out. Even before and after class, there would be a line of people waiting to speak with him. Everyone felt the same thing. He was that teacher we felt safe to share anything with knowing he wouldn't judge. He had this spirit about him that let you know he cared about you, your thoughts, and even your doubts. His class became a safe haven for me.

At the beginning of each class, we'd have a mini devotional. I'd volunteer to help out with either playing the piano, leading the song, saying prayer, sharing a scripture, or bearing testimony. Brother Beebe would leave a few minutes after for anyone else who wanted to share their testimony. I became that one person who without fail would get up to bear testimony. I couldn't help it especially since I felt confident to share it. Brother Beebe left the time open and I would get up and share my memorized testimony. I almost did it every class period. Soon, I started singing church songs and it became a habit for me to always sing as part of my testimony.

It's true when they say you start discovering your testimony in bearing it. Each time I'd share my testimony, I started thinking about what I was actually saying. I was questioning my Primary testimony I learned long ago as a child. Did I really believe those things? Was this church really true? Were the scriptures really the word of God? Many times as I'd bear my testimony, I'd look at Brother Beebe's face and he'd always have a proud, fatherly smile on his face. I think he was praying for me all those times I stood up to speak. He didn't know what I was struggling with, but he made sure that I felt loved and wanted. And I did.

I arrived early to seminary one day. Walking into the classroom, I saw that the desks were pushed toward the walls of the room, and the middle of the classroom was open. In the middle of the room was a projector. Brother Beebe was busy fiddling with it focusing its light on the wall. *Hmm, this should be interesting,* I thought as I looked to find a place to put my backpack down. Brother Beebe greeted me and asked if I could help him with class that day. I was grateful he asked me and nodded yes. He immediately took me to his office. There in his office was a long white dress that appeared to be a wedding dress. I wondered what this dress would be doing in his office. He explained that he needed me to wear the dress and to come out at his signal. I asked him if there was anything else, but that was all he wanted me to do. Puzzled I agreed to help and then he left me in his office to prepare whatever else he needed to get done for his lesson.

As I looked at the dress, I started laughing to myself thinking, *Dang, Brother Beebe! Where'd you find this dress? I mean, it's not that ugly, but it's not even pretty either.* As I lifted the dress investigating its proportions, it looked too big for me. *This must've been in style when the pioneers were still around.* I pulled the dress over my school clothes and was surprised it wasn't as big as I thought it would be. Its length was exactly my height. Looking down at the dress, I was trying to figure out what Brother Beebe's lesson was about. Marriage? Temples? How to not look on your wedding day? I was dumbfounded.

I heard the piano playing. *Oh, they're singing the opening song.* I slowly opened the office door to take a little peek. Everyone was sitting on the ground. *Hmm?* I thought, *What is going on?* I closed the door and sat staring at the dress. Up until this moment, I never really thought or imagined myself being married one day. Most girls think about their wedding colors, the flavor of their cake, how the reception will be decorated, and of course, the dress. They'd dream about the kind of dress they'd like to wear on their wedding day. I, on the other hand, never really thought about those kinds of things because honestly, I didn't know if there would be a guy who would want to marry me. I didn't know if there was anyone who would accept my hands. If I was having a hard time accepting it, then surely, they would be too.

I sat there waiting when the door opened. It was one of my classmates. "You can come out now," he said. Stepping out of the classroom, I could see my classmates faces surprised to see me wearing this white dress. As I walked to the front of the class, I was feeling a little embarrassed. Actually, I felt a lot embarrassed. I caught a glimpse of the temple images the projector projected on the wall. As Brother Beebe continued with his lesson, I grew uncomfortable with everyone looking at me. And even though I tried my hardest not to show it, my ears were burning, my body was sweating, and I knew my oily face was shining bright.

Despite feeling uncomfortable, I started paying attention to the lesson and realized he was speaking of something I didn't expect his lesson to be about: the pioneers. As he shared the miracles the temples brought to the pioneers and of the sacrifices the pioneers made in building them, I forgot about my discomfort and was touched by the stories he shared of their faith and valor. I began to think about my own pioneers.

My parents were pioneers. They both converted to the church and made the trek to Utah, where they found each other. With little knowledge of the English language or the American culture, I could only imagine the trials they faced living in a foreign land. My dad's sole reason to coming to America was to be married in the Salt Lake City Temple. He shared with me his struggle to assimilate to the American culture that humbled him often, but he never lost sight of the temple. The blessings of the temple were reason enough for him to remain faithful to the Lord through his suffering.

As the seminary lesson progressed, I stood there in that white dress feeling a deep sense of gratitude. I felt grateful for the many sacrifices the early pioneers made in establishing the Lord's church on the earth again. I felt grateful for the sacrifices my parents made in obtaining eternal blessings that are only found in the temple. I was so focused on how I looked that I almost missed this spiritual experience and realized that dress I wore symbolized the sacrifices that were made on my behalf. It symbolized the sacrifice the Savior made on my behalf. He prayed for me in the Garden of Gethsemane and carried *my* cross to Calvary; though my sins are as scarlet, they shall be white as snow (see Isaiah 1:18) only through Him and His atoning sacrifice. As I wore that white dress, Brother Beebe provided an opportunity for me to think about things I never thought about before, to see myself in a new way. He invited me to feel something I was struggling with—that I had great worth.

He never forced his beliefs on any of his students, but always left an invitation for us to find out for ourselves. He did just that during our March Madness activities when we were challenged to read from the Book of Mormon cover to cover during the month of March. The last few weeks of February, the Seminary council were advertising the activities they were going to do for March Madness. In the last week of February, Brother Beebe gave us a calendar of March with scriptures on each day to read. We had to check off each day after we read in the scriptures. Every year in Seminary, they would do this activity during March, but I never participated until that year.

When I started the calendar, it was just another thing I had to do every day. I was faithful to the calendar and made sure I read each day's assigned reading. I couldn't wake up earlier in the mornings to read, so I read at night before I went to sleep. That time worked best for me. As we were coming to the end of the Book of Mormon challenge, I started recognizing subtle changes that were happening in my behavior. Before this challenge, I was the angry big sister at home. I'd get so mad if I found my siblings in my room. I was constantly yelling at them, and sometimes for no reason. As the month progressed in my reading, I was starting to notice how calm I felt. I wasn't defensive over everything. I wasn't angry and yelling as much as I did before. I was actually speaking calmly and in a peaceful tone of voice. These small subtle changes to my behavior was a big deal for me.

When the month was over, we had to write in our class journals about the whole experience. Reflecting on the past month, I was astonished at how my behavior changed. I thought maybe it could've been something else, but reading the Book of Mormon was the only thing I did differently the past month. It must be the reason why I was feeling this way. Could it be that this book really is true? I've been taught about this book since I was a little kid. I even said it thoughtlessly so many times in my testimony that I knew the Book of Mormon is the word of God. But was it? Was it really God's words? Remembering what Brother Beebe taught, I decided I needed to pray about it. But I also knew that if I was going to pray about the Book of Mormon, I needed to ask about Joseph Smith. I needed to know for myself if those things were true. If the Book of Mormon was true, then Joseph Smith really did translate it with the power of God given to him.

As I wrote my thoughts about March Madness and the Book of Mormon challenge in my class journal, I decided to pray about everything that day. When I got home, I was trying to figure out when I should pray and decided I'd better wait until bedtime. I was getting ready to go to sleep and as I sat on my bed, I was a bit hesitant to kneel down and pray. All these questions started filling my mind. *Will I be able to hear my answer? What if I don't get an answer? What if Satan comes and gets me? Or better yet, what if an angel appears? That would be so cool,* I thought.

I knelt down on my bed and started praying. I braced myself as I asked my question, and then I waited. Nothing. I thought, maybe if I rephrase my question, I'll get an answer. So I asked again, and still nothing. My head must've lowered with my eyes tightening. I was feeling a bit disappointed when I heard a small quiet voice say, "Fatai, you already know." I perked up a bit, and then I asked if that was my answer. I still got nothing. I took the hint and already knew my answer. Everything was true. Joseph Smith really was a prophet, and the Book of Mormon really is the word of God. Why else would I feel the way I felt when I read it? It literally changed me, and not in a big, over-the-top kind of way, but in the small subtle ways that made such a big impact on me over the course of a month. After my prayer, I felt a sense of peace and knew Heavenly Father heard my prayer. That prayer and the seminary challenge changed the direction of my life.

I wish I could say that after March Madness I became a faithful scriptorian studying the scriptures daily, but I didn't. I went back to my old habits, and I was once again the angry insecure person I was struggling not to be every day. I never forgot the experience, though, and used it as a checkpoint.

We all pass through checkpoints in life. Those checkpoints are the moments when God speaks to you. It's the moments when you feel His love. It's the moments when you feel forgiven for mistakes you've made. It's in the moments when you feel reassured after making a tough decision to keep God's commandments. It's in the moments when you're becoming the person He knows you to be. Those checkpoints are the grace notes that bring meaning to your life, especially when you remember them.

I committed that experience and many others like it to memory. I didn't want to forget those experiences especially the feelings I felt where I witnessed God's power in my life. I prayed earnestly that I would remember it always. It's interesting how in the scriptures, you often read the prophets exhorting us to remember. To remember God's goodness, to remember His sacrifice He made in the garden and on the cross, and to remember God's infinite love for each of us. Because we are human and imperfect, we forget. We forget His goodness. We forget His atoning sacrifice He made for us. We forget His infinite love.

One day, I was angry with Vicelia. I don't remember why, but I was furious. I noticed my scriptures sitting on my dresser and heard a voice say, "Read it." The crazy thing is I didn't think twice and immediately grabbed the scriptures, opened it, and started reading the first thing that caught my eye. After reading the first few words, my anger was gone. *What just happened?* I thought. I continued to read. After finishing that verse, I noticed my anger had completely disappeared. I sat there staring at the pages of the scriptures trying to make sense of what I just experienced. Looking up at the picture of Christ on my wall with a confused look on my face and then back at my scriptures, I was speechless. I remember being taught as a child the power scriptures have and its influence in your life, but to witness and experience this first-hand left me dumbstruck. I haven't forgotten since the powerful influence the scriptures had in my life that day and have since strived to study from them every day.

I've come to know that the scriptures gave me what I was looking for: confidence. For years, I was faking it. I wanted to show desperately that I was confident in my own skin, but I was just arrogant and did my best to hide my insecurities. I was becoming angry with myself because I couldn't fully measure up to where I thought I should be. I had robbed myself in comparison. I thought being confident in oneself is to be loud and boastful, to not be intimidated or appear as weak. But it's the opposite. It's the acceptance of weakness. It's celebrating your differences. It's a firm, sureness of self in all your imperfectness. It's reflecting God's image in your countenance. As I began a frequent study of the scriptures, I started to understand that confidence is the value of trust in its highest form.

I thought I could find confidence only in myself, but I learned that self-confidence could only be found looking outside yourself. I found it in God and I had to learn to trust Him. As I made time to read in the scriptures, I noticed a difference in my day. I was calm. I was more patient. I wasn't defensive or agitated with small things that usually troubled me. Now don't get me wrong, I still would get angry, but I wasn't angry as often as before. I felt confident that my life had purpose. I started recognizing a familiar feeling that I've felt throughout my life even from when I was a child. It was the influence of the Holy Ghost and the scriptures defined its voice clearly for me to understand it has been around me my whole life.

I can remember the first time I felt the Spirit. At the time I didn't know what it was. I was ten years old at the time, listening to the Jets' latest album at the time, Love People. I sat alone in my kitchen listening to each track. They did an arrangement of the hymn, "I Stand All Amazed." As I listened through the first verse, I was overwhelmed with emotion and cried. I didn't fully understand what I was feeling at the time, but I never forgot how I felt. I know now that the Spirit bore witness to me that what I was listening to was true. The message of that song is true.

Two years after that, I was twelve years old and my dad made us go to our rooms and read our scriptures. I could've gone to my room and slept, but I opened my Book of Mormon instead and started reading. As I started reading, not really comprehending what I was reading, I began to feel a warm blanket cover me. I had turned my seventh page when I stopped to recognize the difference I was feeling. I didn't see a blanket with my two eyes, but I felt warm all over as if something was covering me. It felt so good. I went back to reading until I fell asleep. I know now that the Spirit gave me peace and bore witness to me of the power scriptures can have in my life.

With just these few spiritual experiences that I've had, I've tried my hardest not to forget them or the feelings I felt. But when I did, I struggled with finding myself and accepting my hands. Life is hard and it's easy to get caught up in all the negative things that are happening in our lives. Remembering these spiritual moments can give you strength to endure and even look past the negative. But what's even better is actively doing the things that invite the Spirit in your life. When I constantly felt the Spirit's influence, I began to have hope in my future and faith in whatever God had in store for me.

Another grace note in my life has been church leaders who mentored and taught me. When my family moved to the English-speaking ward, I had a hard time at first. Sister Kidd, my young women's leader, must've sensed how out of place I felt moving into the ward. She made sure I felt included in the group. I tried not to like my new ward, but the Lord knew I needed her strong personality to sweep me up, embrace me, and bring me in with the other girls. She trained me to be the leader I needed to be to the girls in my class, and I had many opportunities to lead and serve.

It was not long after that we had a new young women's leader, Sister Croall. She had a nurturing type of personality. She made sure we were active participants in the young women's program. I can still remember her lovingly chastising us girls to stop complaining and get moving. It was the nicest way I ever got in trouble. All I could feel was how she genuinely cared for each one of us. She had us planning our own activities and invited us to teach our class. Sister Croall and Sister Kidd, through their thoughtful guidance, influenced my life positively, providing me opportunities to learn, use, and develop my talents and skills.

Another grace note that continues to impact me is the individuals who have changed the quality of my life with their gifts and talents. Let me tell you about my best friend Meliani. I met Meliani when I was a sophomore. I needed a pianist and my parents had arranged for Meliani to play for me. She's a year younger than I am. It was during our first performance that I recognized her playing style suited my singing. Since that first performance together, I've always turned to her to help me. We began spending a lot of time together practicing for performances. With all the time we spent together, we began to learn more about each other and became friends.

Meliani and I shared a lot in common, but it was in our differences that made our relationship unique. I think that's why we've always gotten along. Her strengths were my weaknesses, and my strengths were her weaknesses. Just in singing alone, our voices are complete opposites. I'm a high soprano and she's a low alto, sometimes even singing tenor. When we started singing together, I recognized how suitable our voices were together. As we started hanging out together outside of music, it strengthened our relationship deeply influencing our music we did together.

Meliani and I were preparing for a fireside featuring the Moleni Brothers. We prepared to perform Jeff Goodrich's song "He Loves Me." Anytime I perform, I try to keep my mind distracted so as to not let my nerves get the best of me. It was hard not to enjoy the powerful spirit the Moleni Brothers brought in their program. When it was my turn to sing, I thought this performance was going to be like any other time. I was wrong.

I stood behind the microphone scanning the crowd for someone I wanted to sing the song to, someone I felt needed the message of the song. Meliani began her intro and I kept searching. There was my cue.

"He loves me . . ."

As I sang those words, something miraculous was beginning to happen and I didn't comprehend it at first what was going on. I continued singing,

". . . more than I know, more than I'll ever understand."

Every word I sang I could hear my voice singing, but I didn't actually feel like I was the one doing the singing.

"He loves me . . ."

It was in that moment I felt like I had stepped away to take a look at myself. There I was listening to myself sing,

"How could He give that love to a broken one like me? And how can He still give that love when I falter so easily?"

As the song progressed, I was overcome with the power of its message. It was me who needed to hear those words. I was singing to myself. I heard His message loud and clear. God indeed loves me. Meliani and I had many faith- and testimony-building experiences together, most of which were experienced through performing.

Our relationship grew when we met Masi. Masi is the brother I never had—and I have three brothers, so that's saying something. He is a man of many talents, but of all the talents he has, Masi is really good at being a friend. He has always been a great example to me of what a good friend should be. So many times he would check in with me unexpectedly, and usually it was at the right time when I needed it most. He always knew the right things to say and even asked some of the best thought-provoking questions that would leave me deep in thought thinking of things I usually don't think about.

We started hanging out with each other and singing more together. It was nice to add Masi in. He completed our harmony.

I'll never forget the first time we really connected and strengthened our friendship. It was during the holidays and our singles ward was going caroling. We were visiting the single adult members who were sick, disabled, or in need of some holiday cheer. The second house we visited was a home of a severely disabled man. As we filled this man's home and started singing, I was overcome with the feelings the Spirit filled that room with. I saw myself as that disabled man and could not hold back my tears.

I excused myself from the room and went to the car. Sitting in the car, I began to weep. I felt so much love. I was overwhelmed with gratitude. Masi and Meliani soon joined me in the car to check on me. As I expressed my feelings, we each opened up sharing our struggles, our insecurities, and appreciation for one another. I was thankful for them that night, and knew our friendship was special. I have never been the same since meeting them.

A final grace note that unexpectedly became a big blessing to me was the One Voice Choir. Ana Tafisi is a local artist I grew up watching perform and I remember being blown away by her talent. After I graduated high school, we became friends and found out we were related. (No surprise there.) She and I were approached from several mutual friends with the idea to make a choir. Given my choir experience in high school and Ana's musical talents, it was an interesting idea, but I felt it wasn't for me. They spoke of other young single adults in the area wanting a place for them to sing. I encouraged them to start one without me. I wasn't really interested in starting a choir because I knew I would have to teach, and teaching takes a lot out of you. I was satisfied with singing my solos here and there, but I soon found myself frequently discussing with my friends about the choir idea. I finally gave in and told them that I was willing to try it out.

Five people showed up at our first practice, but the numbers grew quickly as we began to foster an environment of acceptance and love. It didn't matter if you could sing or not, if you had the desire to sing you were welcome. We soon began to see people from all walks of life coming to choir. With all of our differences, music brought us together and we started to feel "the love of God" within our hearts for each other and for our Savior.

As we thought of names for the choir, a young woman shared a scripture from the Book of Mormon that prompted each of us to examine our own spiritual journey and how it led us there to that very moment. She read, "And they all cried with one voice, saying: Yea, we believe all the words which thou has spoken unto us; and also, we know of their surety and truth, because of the Spirit of the Lord omnipotent, which has wrought a mighty change in us, or in our hearts, that we have no more disposition to do evil, but to do good continually" (Mosiah 5:2).

As we heard this scripture, she suggested the name One Voice, and we unanimously agreed to call the choir One Voice. Many who sat in the room were struggling to stay afloat spiritually. Many were still finding their testimony of the gospel, who were still seeking for direction and purpose to life. Many did not have a relationship with the Savior and felt unworthy of His love. Many wanted a place to develop their talents. And let's be honest—many just came to check out all the other single adults that came. With all the many reasons each person had in coming to choir, it was my prayer that every soul would feel the spirit of the Lord through music. And we did.

We began traveling around the country to perform. With each road trip we made, we began to grow close as a choir family. The choir helped me socially. I became good friends with many people I would've never been friends with had it been for the choir and I genuinely grew a love for them. They had become my family. My high school insecurity of conducting was gone. My choir family supported me and I felt acceptance from them. I reciprocated that love in the way I interacted with everyone. I didn't want anyone to feel what I struggled with for years: to be overlooked and to not be given a chance.

The choir sang some of my original songs. The first song I wrote for the choir was "Come." I was a college student at the time, and I knew we needed some original music and arrangements that would set us apart. I was at school in one of the piano rooms just practicing. I wanted to write a song, but didn't know how or where to start. I decided to pull my scriptures out to do a little study there at the piano.

I began reading several chapters in the Book of Mormon. As I started chapter fifteen of the book of Mosiah, I was impressed with the prophet Abinadi's testimony of the Savior. He was sent to cry repentance to the wicked king Noah, and he did so boldly, even giving his life to seal his testimony. At this time, I was preparing to serve a mission. I thought of my testimony of Christ and the journey I made to know Him. I thought of the long suffering I experienced through my journey of acceptance. And that's when I started to feel a song brewing inside. I didn't know what song it was, but I felt something like a bad itch.

I opened the piano fallboard and started moving my fingers across the black and white keys, randomly pressing a series of different chords. I continued to do this for at least twenty minutes until I felt I found it: the song inside of me. The best way I can describe it is it's a feeling of finally finding something that was lost. Looking over Mosiah 15, Abinadi's testimony brought my song to life:

I would that ye should understand that God himself shall come redeem us.

Dwelling among us the Son of God subjecting himself to the will of the Father.
Were it not for the redemption He made for us that we'll be saved.
For salvation cometh to the world through the Lord but we must heed his words.
He has broken the bands of death, filled with compassion towards His children.

What started out as a difficult, soul-searching endeavor ended up being one of the easiest, freeing experiences I ever had in songwriting. The words of the chorus easily came,

Come heed. Come love. Come to Jesus Christ.
Come willingly to eternal life.
Come feast upon the word of God.
Just trust in Him and come.

When I taught the choir my newly written song, it became our anthem. The song rang true in each of our hearts, and we desired for everyone to feel what we felt. I like to believe we were changed each time we sang Abinadi's testimony. I know I was changed each time I sang about Christ.

With grace notes, it's important to recognize their value and the impact they have in a song. It might not be much, but, oh, how they make a difference. These examples of my grace notes have changed my life for good, and I would not be the person that I am today if it weren't for their influence. "But by the grace of God I am what I am: and his grace which was bestowed upon me was not in vain; but I laboured more abundantly than they all: yet not I, but the grace of God which was with me" (1 Corinthians 15:10).

I still look for grace notes in my life. They remind me of God's love and His watchful care over me. Find your grace notes. Cherish them, because they're God's gift to you—for "the tender mercies of the Lord are over all those whom He hath chosen because of their faith, to make them mighty even unto the power of deliverance" (1 Nephi 1:20). My grace notes came in times I never knew I needed them, and they indeed helped me realize my divine potential as a child of God.

CHAPTER 9

Transpose and Transition

Change is the one thing we can always expect in life. For some, change can be hard. Others handle it with ease. I've learned from experience that change is necessary for progress. Transposing music is just that: change. To transpose a song, you change the key to a higher or lower key from the originating key. When I started transposing my songs, I learned quickly it could only work if each note moved in the same direction and in the same amount of distance. Leave a note behind and it just won't sound the same or have the same effect. Transposing a song adds interest and brings a different energy to the song. I've always liked transposing my songs to highlight the importance of the musical and lyrical content. It's been an expressive tool for me in my songwriting and has taught me how embracing change can greatly bless and beautify your life if you let it.

My last year of high school was so much fun. My senior year, I felt free to be myself. I sang a lot, I taught choir again, and I was heavily involved in student body activities. As the year was coming to an end, I had to decide what I wanted to do after graduation. I stopped pursuing my solo career with the record label. I had plans to attend college to study music. I felt the Spirit of the Lord more, and I looked forward to the future with hope and faith that good things were to come. I had to ask myself important questions. What did I want to do after high school? How did I want to use my talents? I had to examine my life goals, make some new ones, and implement a plan that could help me achieve them.

During lunch one day, I was sitting in the cafeteria with my friends. Graduation day was around the corner, and we were hit with senioritis. We were so ready to be done with school. We started talking about plans we had after graduation. Without even thinking, I blurted out, "I'm going on a mission." I was actually surprised at myself for saying that out loud. Up until that moment, I never thought of going on a mission. I actually didn't think I could go.

Many years prior, my family had the missionaries over for dinner. We hosted a district of missionaries. After dinner, we got to know the missionaries better as we asked them questions about their upbringing and their current mission experience. My mom asked the missionaries if they thought I could go on a mission even with my disability. I'll never forget the surprised look on their faces as they struggled to answer that question. Their district leader carefully responded, "I don't know." As I looked at their faces hearing that answer, I thought, *I wasn't planning on going anyway*, and I never thought about or even considered going on a mission until that day in the cafeteria.

After my surprising declaration during lunch, I began to plan. I was going on a mission. It was all I thought about. One Sunday, I asked to meet with my bishop. During our meeting, I expressed my desire to go on a mission and that I really wanted to be endowed in the temple. He was surprised at my request and chuckled saying I had to wait. That was not what I wanted to hear. I was only eighteen years old, and at the time I had to wait until I was twenty-one to go. I had to wait two years before

I can even start working on my missionary application. But I felt ready. My heart was ready. I was temple ready. I thought going through the temple was the next step to take to get me closer to being a missionary.

I decided to fill my time for the next three years with things that could make time pass by quicker. I traveled more using my dad's flying benefits with Delta. The most exciting place I got to visit was Australia. It was an awesome sight to see the kangaroo passing signs along the roads in the country. Unfortunately, I never got to see one, but I spent majority of my time in the car rides looking for one. My dad's younger sister, Pelenatita, lives there. I had only met several members of her family who came to America, but my visit to Australia would be my first time meeting all nine of her children. I went there for the twenty-first birthday celebration for her oldest child, Nesi.

In the Tongan tradition, a twenty-first birthday is a big coming of age celebration celebrating a woman's virtue and independence. My father had a duty to be the *fa'e huki* for Nesi's twenty-first birthday celebration. In short, the fa'e huki is a position an uncle takes to shows his respect towards his sister and her children; and if the uncle is not present, his children may fulfill that duty. The direct translation of the Tongan word *fa'e* means mother, and the word *huki* means to hold in one's lap. I like to think of the fa'e huki as bodyguards. I had to be Nesi's fa'e huki on behalf of my dad. It was a new experience for me. This custom is all about respect, and I've grown an appreciation for the beauty of the Tongan culture.

My dad's flying benefits allowed me and my family to be there for our extended families and their many occasions and events. I spent a lot of time flying throughout my life, but I also knew since graduating from high school, I needed to do grown-up things. So, I found a job and started working full time. I enrolled in college as a full-time student. I began attending institute classes, which are a lot like seminary classes but on a collegiate level. I spent a lot of time with my friends. I sang more with my friends. I even started the choir One Voice with those friends. I was having fun as I eagerly awaited to start on my mission papers.

When I turned twenty, Edward was nineteen and was preparing to go on his mission. At that time, the age requirements for missionary service was nineteen for boys and twenty-one for girls. I watched the stress my parents had in figuring out how they were going to pay for Edward's mission knowing I was planning to go the following year with Dempsey following shortly after me. My mom was very vocal about her concerns, and I learned that they were trying to figure out a year's worth of having to pay for three missionaries serving at the same time. My dad frequently reassured my mother that there would be a way and wouldn't allow any of us kids to be concerned about money problems.

I had the idea that I could do something with my music and decided to make an album to help my parents pay for our missions. I got to writing original songs. Most of them I wrote while cleaning for my dad's cleaning business. I began creating arrangements to popular hymns and children songs. I was fortunate to have my cousin Leroy help me record and produce the album. He lived out in Arizona, so I made frequent trips throughout the year flying back and forth to record. Most of the original songs were from personal experiences. The one song that was the easiest song for me to write was "My Testimony." When I had to decide what I was going to call the album, it was a no-brainer for me to call it *My Testimony*. Each song reflected a part of my testimony.

As I was meeting with different companies to publish my work, I had reached out to all the copyrights of the hymns and children songs I had recorded. I explained to them my purpose of the album and that all proceeds would go to paying for our missions. They responded by waiving all royalty fees. I was ecstatic and knew this was another blessing the Lord gave me. After I finished recording, I was able to find a publishing company that worked within my budget since I was paying for it out of my own pocket. Everything worked out better than I had planned it, and I was pleased with the end product.

As I look back at the whole process, there were so many blessings and I was able to witness small miracles along the way. It's true when it is said that the Lord will make a way for you, and he did just that many times. I can't count the times I had random thoughts pop in my mind—do this, do that, ask this person, talk to that person, go here, go there—and I would act immediately on those thoughts and would see another piece of the puzzle unfold. This was the workings of the Holy Ghost. Just from the CD project alone, I learned that when you strongly desire something, the Lord's Spirit will inspire and guide your efforts to accomplish it. When I started selling the CDs, I was able to pay for my mission and help my parents with my brothers. That CD is currently being sold online and all proceeds go to the LDS Missionary Fund.

Towards the end of recording, I began to work on my mission papers. That was such a happy day for me. I waited for two years to finally get the missionary application and I treated those papers with the utmost care. I must've gone through it several times in awe that it finally was in my possession. Back then, we were still doing everything on paper and through the postal service, unlike the digital era we are in now. As I finished my missionary application and turned it in, I had finished my

CD project and started selling it. It was an exciting time to get great feedback for my music, but the moment I got my mission call surpassed any joy I had ever felt in my life so far.

The day I got my mission call, I didn't expect it was coming that day. I thought I had to wait another week before it came in my mailbox. It was a Wednesday night, December 13, when my mom asked me if my mission call came in the mail yet. I responded, "No, Mom. It's too early. It's coming next week. They submitted my application last week." My mom asked if anyone checked the mailbox that day, and I told her no. She asked me to get the mail. As I walked towards the mailbox, I saw the big white envelope hanging outside the mailbox.

Grabbing the envelope in disbelief, I checked to see who the envelope was made out to. It was addressed to me, Sister Leslie Fatai, sent from the Church of Jesus Christ of Latter-day Saints. I don't remember how I reacted except that I reacted out of pure joy. My mom said I was jumping around the street like a monkey and hollering like a lunatic. I quickly ran inside the house to escape the cold. I looked at my mom in shock. My mission call was finally here.

I asked my mom if we were going to wait for my dad and sister to come back. My dad and Vicelia were in Tonga at the time. My mom looked deep in thought when she replied, "Let's call Dad." We called my grandma's house in Tonga and got a hold of my dad. As we shared the exciting news, my dad said, "Go ahead. Let's open the call." My mom looked at me to open the call, but I was too excited to read it, so I asked her to open it and read for me. My mom opened the envelope and started reading my letter out loud:

"Dear Sister, you are hereby called to serve as a missionary for The Church of Jesus Christ of Latter-day Saints. You are assigned to labor in the Texas Houston East Mission . . ."

I was so excited to hear Texas that I forgot where Texas was located. Through my shock, my mom continued to read that I would be preaching the gospel in the Spanish language. I was stunned at the news. I went to my room and offered a prayer of gratitude for this new opportunity to grow and change. I felt a reassurance that Texas was where I needed to be. But I only had one request: I wanted to know at least one person from home.

I shared the news with my family and friends. I was to enter the Missionary Training Center (MTC) in two months' time. It's always nice to have others be happy for you and share in your joy. That's what makes having good friends a blessing. They're there to lift you up when you're falling, and they're there to celebrate with you in all your achievements. Preparing for my farewell date, the moment I had been waiting almost three years for, had finally come. I would finally get to go through the temple.

Everything we do in the Church points to the temple. The temple is a sacred place of worship and is the house of the Lord. Remember those priesthood keys I spoke about? The restoration of the Gospel of Jesus Christ brought forth priesthood keys authorizing The Church of Jesus Christ of Latter-day Saints to carry forth the Lord's work of salvation for all of God's children from past, present, and future. This work happens in the temple.

The Savior taught His Apostles, "I will give unto thee the keys of the kingdom of heaven: and whatsoever thou shalt bind on earth shall be bound in heaven" (Matthew 16:19). With those priesthood keys, we are able to participate in sacred ordinances making covenants towards salvation even exaltation in life after death. This gives us the opportunity to live with and even become like our Heavenly Father. All of this is dependent on our faithfulness and worthiness to keep those sacred covenants throughout our mortal life.

I entered the temple on my twenty-first birthday. I had taken temple classes to prepare for this day. People expressed their excitement for me and recommended I keep an open mind and to focus on my feelings and on any spiritual impressions I'd receive. If I can describe my temple experience in one word it would be *solemn*. I felt a profound sense of peace walking inside the temple seeing everyone dressed in white. It truly felt like heaven. My experience that day was life-changing, and I've never been the same since.

Several weeks later, I was to enter the MTC. Many of my friends came with my family to see me off. As I said my good-byes to my friends and family, I was too excited to cry. They knew it too as I happily hugged each one of them. I gave a hearty, "See you next year!" and walked away. I was ready to be a missionary.

The MTC was a great experience. I gained a lot of weight, which was new for me. It was a welcoming change, although my clothes didn't agree. I started out with one companion, Sister Goode, and ended my time there with two. Sister Jenkins joined our companionship and balanced us out perfectly. It was hard at first getting used to not being alone all the time. We always had to be with our companions, and sometimes I would forget. But being with my companion grew on me, and after my mission, it was hard to adjust being alone again. My MTC companions and I were going to Houston together, and we were eager to get out in the field. I had some of the best instructors who really challenged us to deepen our conversion and testimonies of Christ.

Learning Spanish was hard. My tongue grew accustomed with Spanish pronunciation since it shares similarities with the

Tongan language, but the *gramática* of Spanish was where I struggled. All I can say is the gift of tongues is real, y'all. I think it's harder to learn a foreign language in a stateside mission because you're not fully enveloped in the culture and language. This only meant I had to work harder with my Spanish. Some days we'd try to have a language fast and only speak Spanish. This was hard especially when we'd pass by people who only spoke English. But the Lord knew our desires and pulled through for us when we needed to share truths of the gospel.

When I first arrived in Houston, I was overwhelmed with the humid heat. I've only lived in Utah's dry heat so when we arrived late in spring, I couldn't believe how hot it was. I seriously didn't know how I was going to survive that summer if it was already that hot. My mission president, Michael Lake, and his assistants picked us up from the airport and treated us to some authentic Texas BBQ. Texas doesn't play around when it comes to that good ol' Southern comfort food.

We soon were at the mission home and met President Lake's wife. I was deeply impressed with some things they shared with us that changed my perspective on missionary work. President Lake shared how throughout our missions we will meet all kinds of people, but it's understanding the reason and purpose behind meeting that person. I was lost in my thoughts as I thought of the souls I was meant to meet in Texas that only I could reach because of my personality, testimony, or specific talents that I had. I also thought of the souls who I needed to meet to teach me and help me learn whatever God wanted me to learn from this mission experience. I kept this in mind with every companion, mission leaders, ward members and leaders, and everyday people I met in Texas.

Time on the mission is divided by transfers. A transfer is six weeks long. My first transfer began my first day in Texas.

We were to meet our trainers that night. I was eager to meet my trainer. When we arrived in the chapel, we went to a room where our missionary trainers were waiting for us. Approaching the room, I recognized one of the trainers standing at the door. It was Elenoa, a friend from home. She was known as Sister Fuka on the mission. I embraced Elenoa and immediately remembered my prayer. The Lord heard my simple request and I saw my friend from home.

Feeling grateful, I was eager to see what else the Lord had in store for me. Whoever trained me was going to be someone who will set the tone for the rest of my mission. I fully trusted in the selection process and I looked forward to meeting her. As my name was called, I learned I had not one but two trainers. I was deeply grateful. Lord knew I would need the help, and how lucky I was to have two examples to learn from. Looking back, I could've reacted negatively and took it offensively, but I saw the positive. President Lake's words from earlier that day had prepared me for that moment and many moments after throughout my mission.

My trainers were Sister Hansen and Sister Okada. They had been companions during the last transfer and were now training together. It so happened that my first transfer was also Sister Hansen's last transfer. My first week with them was busy-busy thanks to all their hard work the last transfer. We had a baptism my first Saturday. Rogelio had been their investigator for some time and had now committed to being baptized. Meeting all the people they had been teaching for weeks was a lot of fun.

Watching my trainers teach was overwhelming at times because I had a hard time understanding the Spanish. So many times I thought to myself, *What type of Spanish is this? This isn't what I learned in the MTC.* That first transfer I can remember many times being spoken to or asked a question in Spanish and I would just smile and nod my head yes like a total idiot. Thankfully, my companions would notice the lost look on my face and would translate for me. Did I mention that I had a hard time dealing with Houston's heat? I don't know how many times I must've dozed off during appointments. The heat can do that to you, especially when you're not physically fit.

Because I struggled to speak Spanish, I could've easily been down on myself, but thankfully my companions were inspired and used my strengths to contribute in our lessons. I never felt left out. They always offered me the opportunity to practice my Spanish. They made sure I had a part in the lessons whether it was teaching a principle or sharing a scripture. When they found out I played the piano, I became the ward pianist during church meetings. My trainers volunteered me to help out with any music in the ward. I appreciated that because I felt useful despite not knowing the language or knowing anyone. It was nice feeling needed.

My favorite thing they'd always let me do was sing. I sang a lot on my mission. From the moment my trainers heard me sing, they had me sing all the time. I didn't realize it at first, but my confidence grew each time I sang. Singing in Spanish also helped me with the language. Using music was the best way I could serve, and it opened opportunities for me to utilize my musical talents. Throughout my mission, we hosted musical firesides that allowed missionaries, members, and nonmembers to share their testimony of Christ through spoken word and song. Despite all the struggles I experienced, I felt validated each time I used my talents for the Lord.

Before the mission, I had been in the darkness for too long. And now that I fully stepped into the light, I felt empowered to do anything that the Lord asked of me. I learned quickly that missionary work is hard work. It is not for the faint of heart. At times you will be asked to do hard things that might leave you feeling uncomfortable and even discouraged. Riding a bike was that hard thing for me.

It had been over ten years since I rode a bike. My first area was a bike area, and bicycling was our main mode of transportation. I was able to have custom high-rise handlebars added to my bike which made riding more comfortable for me since my arms are short. But even with my special handlebars, I was still trying to get used to riding a bike in a skirt. The first time I fell off the bike, I slowed down too late at a street corner. My fingers weren't strong enough to pull on the brakes quickly. I always had to get a head start on pulling the brakes just so I could stop when I needed to.

Many times as I rode the bike, I knew people were staring at me. For the longest time in my life, I had struggled with people staring at me. It led me to a depression that paralyzed my faith and hope to where I even considered suicide as a freshman in high school. Riding a bike in a skirt was begging for attention. My hands were drawing attention. But being a missionary on the Lord's errand and exposing myself in this way, I gladly rode my bike each day because I knew I was riding for Jesus. Cheesy, huh? I knew my discomfort was nothing compared to what the Savior experienced, so I was willing to be uncomfortable for Him.

Midway through my mission, I got into a bad bike accident. One of my brakes was already out and no longer worked, so I was riding with only one good brake. I had ignored the promptings to fix it, and I thought I would be okay if I rode my bike carefully. We were on our way home one day and rode down a steep hill. As my bike accelerated, I tried to slow down but my one brake was not strong enough to slow down. My hands lost control of the handlebars, and I swerved right into the ditch, flying over the bike into the shrubbery on the side of the street. I could not feel my body. I lay there for a good thirty minutes until I was able to gather some strength to move. I slowly got up, and we made our way to a member's home nearby. My zone leaders came to our rescue giving me a blessing of healing before driving us home.

The next day we headed to the clinic to get me checked out by a doctor. Thankfully, I didn't break anything, but my body was sorely bruised, and my face was swollen with a few cuts and scrapes. The doctor prescribed me some pain medication and ordered me to rest up. My body was going to be in severe pain for the next twenty-four hours. I took the pain medication when the pain became unbearable and I grew extremely drowsy. It knocked me out completely. I stayed home for a couple days to recover.

It was hard being stuck inside. I felt bad for my companion, who stayed home with me. We had some really great people we were teaching at the moment, and it was frustrating for me that we had to cancel some of our appointments. I regret not listening to the still small voice that told me to fix my brakes. In the end, I paid the price with my own body and we lost precious time to preach the gospel.

At the beginning of my time with any new companion, we openly discussed my needs. Fixing my hair was my main request. Even before the mission, I knew that I was going to need help fixing my hair, especially since it's hot in Texas. Back home, that was the one thing my sisters helped me with. I hoped and prayed that all my companions would help me and thankfully they did. But as they did, I learned a few things that changed my perspective on charity.

Every morning as I got ready for the day, my companion helped me put my hair in a simple ponytail. Fortunately, all my companions knew how to do a ponytail. There were times when the ponytail was not up to my standards, but I began to experience something that even my sisters hoped I would've learned long ago. Before the mission, I was a perfectionist when it came to my hair. Nothing seemed good enough. I used my hair as an excuse to cover up what I was really struggling with: the acceptance of my limitations. But when I had a bad hair day on the mission, I started looking past the imperfect ponytail, and began to experience the true nature of this simple service that had been rendered to me daily.

Midway through my mission, I got to serve again with my MTC companion Sister Jenkins for one transfer. Since we had served together before, she already knew what I needed help with. A couple weeks into our transfer, we had a falling out one morning. We had finished our studies and planning for the day and got into a heated discussion. We had to leave soon to avoid being late. Without resolving the contention, we gathered our things and prepared to head out. My companion came into the room I was in and asked if she could help me do my hair. I was taken aback by her request. I'm usually the one asking for help, but she came and she asked *me*. Surprised by her question, I silently wept, nodding a yes. I thought, *How could she still want to help me fix my hair? She doesn't have to help me and, yet, here she is.* My heart was softened.

That day, I learned an important lesson: Charity, when given sincerely, changes hearts and transforms lives. Sister Jenkins showed me what charity looked like. I used to not like being on the receiving end of an act of service. I wanted to be the giver because I didn't want to appear weak or needy. This simple service my companions did for me each day taught me that it's important to not only give service to others, but to gratefully and humbly receive it as well. When you do so, you grow closer to God. Who would've thought a simple ponytail would teach me some of life's greatest lessons on acceptance and charity?

The last area I served in was an area called Denver Harbor. This area had been covered by elders—male missionaries—for years and had the reputation of being a dangerous area. It was closed for a period of time until my mission president felt inspired to bring in sister missionaries. Sister Okada and Sister Jenkins got transferred there and reopened the area. I got moved there the next transfer and served with Jenkins. I served in Denver Harbor for the last four transfers of my mission. Three of those transfers I served with Sister Waddoups.

Denver Harbor was the hardest area I ever served in. Spending six months in that area, you would think I had a lot of baptisms, but I didn't. We only had one during that whole time. I learned quickly from my time there that I was sowing little seeds of faith in the lives of those who resided there. I constantly reminded myself the counsel President Lake gave on my first day in Texas and I treated each encounter as heaven sent. I could only trust and have faith that those seeds of faith we planted would someday grow into sacred covenants made through sacred ordinances of the gospel.

At the end of my mission, I had an exit interview with my mission president before returning home. He asked me to summarize my mission in one sentence. Without hesitation I responded, "Your attitude makes all the difference." I enjoyed being a missionary because I chose to. There was always something to learn from each experience. The Spirit I constantly felt as a missionary was a privilege.

The Apostle Paul wrote to the Colossians, "As ye have therefore received Christ Jesus the Lord, so walk ye in him" (Colossians 2:6). My mission transposed me to a better way of life because it strengthened my relationship with Jesus Christ. I felt closest to Him as I walked in His footsteps. I came to know Him personally through my missionary service. The mission changed my attitude and my perspective on life. I felt happier.

Being a missionary taught me that everything I did for the Lord mattered and it would be accounted for. I may not have seen immediate results, but I knew the Lord saw my heart and knew my intentions. In life, we experience expected or unexpected changes. Keeping your sights on the Lord will always lead you closer to Him; and as you come unto Him, He will help you transition and adjust to His light and blessings that will fill your life as you come unto Him.

CHAPTER 10

Sustain Me

When I started playing the piano, I noticed a big difference when I used the sustain pedal. Have you ever noticed the foot pedals at the bottom of a piano? Each pedal has a function that affects the sound. The pedal furthest to the right is my favorite: the sustain pedal. If I don't use the sustain pedal, the music my five fingers play sounds choppy and disconnected. Using the sustain pedal allows the music to continue even after I've let go of the keys and moved on. The pedal is true to its name. It supports the music until its vibration has stopped or the pedal is released completely. The pedal makes up for what I lack, and I am able to focus on what I do have to express the music inside me.

Throughout my life, I received constant support from God, family, and great friends that sustained me through my struggles. Although at times I felt alone, I really wasn't. I just chose to see my solitude and failed to recognize all the little tender mercies the Lord sent my way. As we experience challenges in our lives, the Lord sustains us as we walk by faith having hope in our hearts that things will get better. And they do. Failure to see it causes more distress and suffering. Trust me, I know. As I've grown and moved forward in life, it is apparent I did not make this journey alone. Hence, I refuse to forget what has remained constant in my life and seek to acknowledge and count my blessings.

I came home a different person after serving a mission. I was spiritually sensitive to my surroundings and had to reacquaint myself with home. Home for the past year and a half was in Texas, and returning to my first home felt foreign. I was surprised at the many things that bothered my spirit. For one, I did not like loud music. We were driving home one day when my siblings were blasting their pop music. I immediately felt uncomfortable. It was unsettling. The song wasn't swearing. It was just your typical love pop song. I was surprised at how I felt and asked them to turn down the music.

It is common for returned missionaries to notice a decreased influence of the Spirit a full-time mission brings. I soon began to notice my spiritual sensitivity was declining. The difference in my environment slowly started to affect my spirit, and I was beginning to feel empty. As a full-time missionary, you're busily working, serving, and helping those in need. You fully immerse yourself in Christ and strive to exemplify Him through your being. But when I came home, I had a lot more time on my hands and I was bored.

The mission was the first time I felt completely comfortable in my own skin. But now that I was experiencing these unwelcome feelings, I feared that I might regress to that dark hole I struggled for years to get out of. The immense blessings and life-changing experiences I had on the mission revealed the cure that saved me from my long struggle with low self-esteem and depression: service. I needed to start actively serving and I prayed to know where and how I could do it.

I started filling my time with purposeful activities. Thanks to the planning skills I acquired on the mission, I began planning my days, weeks, and sometimes months with meaningful activities that would keep me on the path towards progress. The first thing I decided to do was renovate my room. If I was going to make some changes in my life, my room needed one too. I began looking at colors I wanted to paint my walls and decided on a sage-green color. I had my work cut out for me and started ripping out my carpet and cleaned the hardwood floor underneath. I painted my walls, varnished my wood floors, and organized my room. Pleased with the changes, it became easier for me to tackle my goals.

I enrolled in school and waited for classes to begin. In the meantime, I needed to find something to fill my time with. I started applying for jobs in hopes to start working. I was going to need the money to pay for school. I got a job at the post office. One day as I was out doing some errands, I drove by the hospital near my house. As I drove past, I heard these words come to my mind, "You should volunteer there." I got home and went online to see if I could volunteer there and was happy to learn I could. I called the number listed for inquiries and was asked to come in to fill out an application and meet for an interview.

I soon found myself at the hospital filling out the application waiting for an interview. Meeting with the interviewer, she asked me what brought me there to volunteer. Without thinking, I said, "Honestly, I have a lot of time on my hands right now. I need something good to do." After I said that, I thought maybe I should've been more thoughtful with my response. I began to worry that maybe they wouldn't let me volunteer, but I was relieved when she asked me about my availability. I soon received my uniform and a schedule and left for home grateful I had listened to that prompting.

I chose to help out at the front desk. I was the guide answering questions, directing people, offering wheelchairs and other services to patrons, and checking people in for outpatient services. Volunteering in the hospital is something I wish I had done before my mission. Thanks to the hospital's quiet environment, I was able to get a lot of homework done during some down time. Volunteering in the hospital brought a familiar spirit I felt often on the mission.

As I began filling my time with volunteering, school, and work, I also filled my time with service opportunities within the church. I was serving at the time on my stake's Primary board as the music leader. I loved that calling as I shared my testimony through music. We frequently made visits to all the different ward primaries of the stake. I was visiting a Primary in Salt Lake City. As their Primary president introduced me and gave me time to speak to the children, I was surprised at what I was seeing and hearing. Several loud Primary children were mimicking my hands with their hands and started making fun of me saying very rude and disrespectful things. It didn't bother me as much as it bothered their leader. What happened next taught me how to sustain your leaders.

Their sweet Primary president interrupted me as she stopped the disrespectful kids and their negative behavior. She came up and stood beside me. We stood together in silence for a minute and then she emotionally began to take that moment to teach her Primary children. As I stood there in awe of the whole situation, I came to realize I was meant to be there as the subject matter of an important lesson her Primary children needed to learn. But it went deeper than that. As I stood there looking at these children, I felt no ill will towards them. Instead, my heart was full of sorrow and compassion.

I began to feel hope for them as I saw a glimpse of who I used to be, and silently prayed that if they kept coming to church, they might experience what I did: the life-changing power of the gospel of Jesus Christ. I could only imagine how the Savior must have felt as he was scorned, spit upon, beaten. And after all his suffering and pain, he forgave his trespassers "for they know not what they do" (Luke 23:34). I was grateful to be there with that Primary that day. The Lord needed me to teach an important lesson to those children. Now I don't know if those children changed their behavior, but I do know that me being there affected at least one person: me.

In our lives, we may experience things we have no control over, but I've learned that God is an all-wise, powerful, and loving God who sees a bigger picture—a better picture. Sometimes in life you'll be put in positions where you'll be ridiculed and mocked just for being you, but I can say for myself that it was during those moments I felt closest to God. It's hard to see it, but the Lord is with you, sustaining you especially in your suffering. Please don't forget that.

When I came home from the mission I had a new bishop, Bishop Chestnut. He was our first home teacher when we moved to the neighborhood ward. He took good care of us and made the transition from the Tongan ward to the English ward better than we expected. He was a really good friend to my family. He would always greet me with, "Hey, girlfriend," and I'd always crack up laughing. He had a way of making people feel comfortable around him.

Bishop Chestnut asked to meet with me after church one day. I was curious to know what it was about. He offered me an opportunity to serve in the temple as a volunteer. I was overwhelmed because I had prayed for opportunities to serve, but never considered serving in the temple. Gratefully, I accepted the opportunity and soon I was meeting with temple personnel discussing my schedule to serve in the temple.

I initially thought if I filled my time with good things that I'd be proactively serving like how I did on the mission, but I began to have too many things on my plate and I was feeling overwhelmed. But with all the things I filled my time with, serving in the temple became my saving grace. The temple's quiet and peaceful environment allowed me to disconnect from the world and reconnect with God on a deeper, spiritual level. It was a time for me to recharge my battery, and I began to see blessings from my service there. The biggest blessing? I did not go insane from the crazy, hectic schedule I created for myself.

When you're overwhelmed and worn out, you're not performing at 100 percent. I began to see it affect every aspect of my life. I was running late to everything. I couldn't keep all my commitments. I wasn't giving my best efforts. I began feeling guilty all the time for not meeting this high bar of expectation I had set for myself. And in order to redeem myself, I would add an extra thing to do on my to-do list, thus widening the gap between my expectations versus my reality. I recognized that I had to let go of some good things to focus on the best things for me. I had to simplify my life, straighten my priorities, and focus on the things that mattered most.

But I have a confession to make. I used everything that I had going on in my life as an excuse to avoid the one thing that a return missionary should think about: marriage. My last transfer on the mission, I shared my concerns with my companion about dating. I was not looking forward to dating. I wished that I could skip that step and just get to the married part and start a family.

What I feared most about dating was acceptance. I had struggled to accept my hands for years and the thought of someone else accepting my hands and even wanting to be married to me did not seem practical. So, when I came home from the mission I was anti-social. Obviously, I couldn't be antisocial for long with all the activities I was involved in. And truthfully, it was hard for me to do anyway because I've always enjoyed socializing with others. The pressure to date when I finished my mission was really heavy that I felt uncomfortable being around other young adult men my age.

I had only been home for a couple of weeks when my friends from One Voice Choir asked me to help them in a fireside they were doing in Sacramento, California. I initially refused them when I learned it was for a young single adult conference, but they were persistent in asking until I gave in and said yes. The day of the fireside, I flew out to Sacramento.

The music performed that night gave me exactly what I needed: confidence to face my fear of dating. As I played the piano and sang throughout the fireside, I felt once again my worries and insecurities replaced with faith and hope. The Spirit of the Lord used the power of music to remind me of God's plan for me. I was reminded of God's love that has sustained me throughout my life. I needed to believe that the Lord's choice blessings were available to me—even marriage to a man who would love me for me accepting all of my imperfections. I just needed to trust in the Lord and hope I would recognize that man.

After that fireside, I was open to meeting people and decided to transfer my church membership records to the singles ward. As I met different guys and went on dates, I realized there was something I was looking for in particular. I didn't know exactly what it was or how to describe it except that it was a feeling I knew I would recognize the moment I felt it. I had to walk by faith and make sure I was living worthy of the influence of the Holy Ghost. I depended on the Lord's Spirit, not to do everything for me, but to send me confirmations along the way. I eventually discovered what I was looking for through someone I least expected.

Let me tell you about Ofa. Fun fact: *Ofa* in Tongan means "love." I met Ofa through One Voice Choir. He moved to Utah from California and lived with his cousins. I knew his cousins and grew up with them in the same ward. His cousins brought him to choir practice one day. We became acquainted, and we only said "hi" and "bye" to each other. Nothing more.

We never had an actual conversation until three years later. I had been home from the mission for six months when he decided to call me out of the blue. I was at a friend's house working on some music when I received his phone call. What impressed me the most from our conversation was how easy it was to talk to him.

We spoke as if we knew each other well. I felt comfortable speaking with him. I was even more surprised when he asked me out on a date. Impressed by our conversation and with his boldness to ask me out, I told him yes. So, we planned to meet later that night. I let him know I was going to bring my sister and told him he was welcome to bring a cousin or friend along.

Later that day, we met at a restaurant and had dinner. That feeling was there again throughout the date. I felt at ease talking with him and just being around him. It was nice to not feel the pressures of dating and pretending to be something you're not. I felt good about myself being around him. He left back to California the next day and we wouldn't be in contact with each other for several weeks.

Ofa called me up about a month later just to check up on me, and soon we were having daily conversations over the phone. I learned that we shared a lot in common. We're

Tongan-American. We're the oldest child in our families. We were born and raised in the LDS faith. And we both liked to sing, just to name a few.

I enjoyed our conversations, and I started having feelings for him. I didn't realize it at first, but as our relationship progressed, I realized that what I was looking for was inside me the whole time. It took someone like Ofa to make me feel comfortable in my own skin. All this time I worried about no man being able to accept and love me for me, when really it was myself who still needed to accept the truth that I am worth being loved. I deserve to be loved, but it all needed to start with me. Ofa, without even knowing it, lived up to his name and taught me to love myself as he loved me.

My parents were noticing my daily phone calls with Ofa and were not surprised when I started asking them if we were related, because I did not want to date my own cousin, which is a common problem Tongans have, because let's face it—all Tongans, and Polynesians in general, are related somehow. But my dad reassured me we weren't, and we continued to have our daily phone calls.

Ofa was planning to come to Utah soon with his family for general conference, and we decided to go on a date when he got into town. I'll never forget that when he came to pick me up, he brought flowers for my mom and some chocolates for me. He definitely won some brownie points with my mom. He met my dad briefly, and then we were off on our date. It was during our date that we decided to date exclusively, but there was a catch. Ofa had to ask my dad for permission to date me.

The next day, Ofa was at my house talking with my dad. He asked my dad if he could date me, and thankfully my dad said yes, but he had one condition: I could not go alone with Ofa without someone with me at all times. That someone would be my brother Ekuasi. He was sixteen years old at the time. Ofa agreed to my dad's conditions, and we were excited to officially be dating. After my dad gave his consent, he gave us counsel that made us seriously think about our possible future together.

My dad spoke to each of us plainly. He instructed us to get to know each other and find out if we really wanted to be together. He told Ofa, "Don't waste your time with my daughter if you feel she's not the one you want to be with. Go find yourself another girl." He looked at me and said, "The same goes for you too. Don't waste each other's time." My dad's words caused us to think about each other and we had to search deep within our hearts what we truly felt.

Because of my busy schedule, our time together was limited, so Ofa would join me whenever I was free. The following day Ofa came with me to support my brother Edward and Snow College's Luau. Edward was one of the many students dancing. He asked Vicelia and me to help out with a Hawaiian number as part of intermission during the show. The performances turned out great, the food was bomb, and the luau ended a success.

Ofa and I had a two-hour drive back home. I'll never forget that drive because it was the first time Ofa held my hand, and it was the fingers-interwoven-together kind of holding hands. Let. Me. Tell. You. It was so awkward for me, and he knew it too. I tried to pull my hand away several times, but he wouldn't let go and he tightened his grip. I expressed how weird it was for me to have him hold my hand, and I'll never forget his words to me. He said, "Fatai, your hands are perfect!" Yeah, I just about melted. He had completely won me over.

Two days later, it was finally conference weekend. I really wanted to go to the temple, and I was grateful Ofa came with me. As we served in the temple that beautiful Friday morning, we made our way to the celestial room to pray. Sitting there, holding hands, I felt completely at peace with myself and with Ofa. We had fallen in love and in a short amount of time. Everything between us fell so easily into place. As I looked to Ofa, he met my gaze and asked, "Marry me?" The funny thing is I was not surprised with this question. We wanted to be with each other and it only felt natural for us to take the next step and get married. So, when he popped the question, I nodded without hesitation yes. Did he have a ring when he proposed? No. Did I care about having a ring? No. Do I currently wear a wedding ring? No. We did get rings when we got married, but I told him I don't wear rings. That's just my preference, and I knew he was a keeper when he supported me.

Our relationship escalated within one week. We went from dating exclusively at the beginning of the week when he arrived to Utah from California to getting engaged at the end of the week. It was exciting for us to share our joy as we announced our engagement to our friends and family. We set the wedding date to take place in a little over four months. Yes, I said four months. But with everything happening so quickly, I never second-guessed my decision to marry Ofa. He was the answer to a prayer I didn't know I had been carrying inside my heart for quite some time. That prayer was a hope I had in my heart and I was grateful that little glimmer of hope became a reality.

Several weeks before the wedding day, my dad and I were sitting in the kitchen talking. He asked me, "Fatai, are you ready to be married?"

Without thinking, I replied, "I'm as ready as I'll ever be, Dad."

He began to share with me his experience of meeting Ofa on the day he came to take me out on our first official date. He said, "When I saw Ofa come inside the house, I saw the faces of his family that took me into their home many years ago when I got baptized to the church. My dad kicked me out of the house and I had nowhere to go, but they took me in and loved me. I saw their faces in Ofa's face that day, and I knew I was going to love this guy." I couldn't help but smile.

He continued to ask me, "Do you love Ofa?"

Surprised by his question I said, "Well, yes, Dad. Why else would I be marrying him?"

He then paused to think and asked, "Do you feel like you know Ofa?"

I carefully thought of my answer and said, "Honestly, no. There's still a lot I have to learn about him, and there's a lot he still has to learn about me. We just started dating, got engaged in one week, and now we're about to be married in just a couple of weeks. There's definitely a lot we don't know about each other, but I expect us to fight and to struggle as we learn to live with each other. I look forward to it, but I also know that we'll grow together and help each other out."

A friend of mine asked me when she found out about my engagement, "How did you know that he was the one?"

I could only reply, "I just know."

Puzzled, she did not look satisfied with that response. I've thought a lot about it and I realized that I knew he was the one because I chose him to be the one. But let's be real for just a second. If I decided to not marry Ofa, I might've married someone else and said that he was the one. But it's more than just finding the one that's the cutest or the richest or the smartest. It's all about commitment.

It's finding someone you want to commit yourself to knowing even after an argument you'll still feel genuine love for that person. It's finding someone who can accept your stinky bad breath in the morning and still want to kiss you. It's finding someone who can still see the good in you even after you've messed up. It's finding forgiveness for that someone who might forget what you like or dislike. It's remembering why you chose your partner in the first place when you begin to doubt your love. I knew I was ready to marry Ofa because I finally found someone who was worth committing myself to, who I wanted to experience life with, the good, the bad, and all the in-betweens. I wanted to marry Ofa and couldn't imagine my life without him.

Ofa moved back to Utah for school at Utah Valley University for the summer, and we had the summer to plan the wedding. Throughout the whole wedding experience, we were very blessed to be surrounded by the many hands who sustained, nurtured, taught, raised, and befriended us throughout our lives. All the things that really mattered to us on our big day happened perfectly. I was overwhelmed by the support. *Have I always been this blessed?* It was a blessing to see the faces of those who impacted my life for good, who lifted me up when I felt down on myself, who comforted me when I felt broken, and encouraged me to press forward with faith come and celebrate with me and Ofa on our special day. Being sealed to Ofa in the temple was the highlight for me as we were promised some amazing blessings if we kept our promises to each other and to God.

After the wedding, the part I looked forward to the most would be some of the most challenging, soul-searching, fulfilling years of my life. Marriage is not for the weak. Marriage is not meant to be done on a whim. Marriage is not perfect. It's hard work, but it's worth it. Marriage exceeded my expectations 1,000 percent. The joys are beyond what I could've imagined, and the sorrows redefined what low meant. In my time of being married, the one thing that sustained me through it all is Christ and His gospel teachings.

One day, Ofa and I had an argument. It was over something so trivial that I can't even recall what our argument was about. Ofa left to school, and I was left at home getting ready for work. Feeling suffocated from my frustration, I knelt down to pray to rid myself of the contention I felt. I remember specifically asking in my prayer, "I don't know what to do, Lord," when immediately I heard loud and clear, "Love him." I paused to think about what I just heard. A calm and peaceful feeling overcame me. I knew then I needed to love him, but how was the question.

As I was driving home from work, I was lost in my thoughts. During my shift, I spent a lot of time reading and listening to the scriptures. I pondered a lot on my answer to love him when the thought came to *love God*. I was a bit confused. How can I love Ofa by loving God? Ofa's not God. I started pondering on those two words: love God. What did that mean to me? I thought, well, loving God is keeping His commandments. It's keeping the promises I made at baptism and in the temple. Loving God meant to follow the Savior's example, to have patience, humility, and forgiveness. Loving God meant being the person He knew me to be by using my talents to serve those in need. Loving God is loving my neighbor and recognizing that we are all children of God.

In that very moment, I began to see clearly the relationship between Ofa and God. Ofa is a child of God. Heavenly Father loves him. I know that. But if I am to love Ofa, only Heavenly Father would know how because He's the only one I know that loves my husband completely, especially with all his shortcomings and weaknesses. I learned that loving God is in fact loving

Ofa, and I was able to be better in loving my husband as I loved the Lord, with all my heart, soul, and mind.

Even though at times I felt alone, God has never left my side. When I let go of His teachings, like the sustain pedal, He held the music out long enough for me to return to His warm embrace. I know there were times where He stepped aside for me to learn what I needed to learn, to become who I needed to be. We come to this mortal experience to learn and unlock the divine potential that resides deep within each of us. Through trials and tribulations, we discover who we truly are by exemplifying our Savior through our thoughts, our words, and our deeds. Learning to recognize those blessings that sustain us empowers us to continue forward with faith in God's plan.

CHAPTER 11

Finding My Heart Song

Being a pianist, I didn't have to deal with tuning my instrument like my other musician friends did. I quickly learned it makes all the difference in your song if your instrument is in tune or not. Tuning your instrument is all about adjusting it to the correct pitch. Once I had to perform on an old out-of-tune piano. I was unprepared for the change of key I had to sing in. The piano keys were old and stiff, and some didn't even work. My performance turned out okay, but I'll never forget how sore my fingers felt after playing that piano. I had to make an adjustment of my own that day to play my song, and my fingers found a hidden strength that day to play those old rickety keys.

When I started writing music, I always felt a song inside my heart. Sometimes I could hear a melody, other times it was just words, but I would always have this itch I needed to get out of my system. There were times where I was close to finishing a song, and I would feel stuck because it just didn't feel right. Most of the time what I needed was an adjustment. That adjustment was all about fine-tuning the soul of the song.

Fine-tuning my music has taught me how important it is for us to be in tune with the Lord. Our lives become out of tune with God when we don't adjust to the constant change life brings. We become so out of tune with Him that we forget the words of life. We forget the sound of His voice. We forget the rhythm that our soul longs for. We become lost and can no longer hear the music. We need to realign ourselves to God's frequency to hear the music again.

We come to this earth to perform a song so to speak. That song is our purpose in life. For some, it'll be easy to hear, and for others, it'll take a lifetime to find. In finding your heart song, you find out who you are and what you were meant to do. But this also depends on your listening skills and how in tune you are with your heart and with His.

God is like the songwriter. He knows your song. He created it and has entrusted it to you. Born from the songwriter's heart, your song was given as a gift to you to figure out how it should sound.

This mortal life allows us to learn important lessons needed for our eternal well-being for "this life became a probationary state; a time to prepare to meet God; a time to prepare for that endless state" (Alma 12:24). Each one of us is born imperfect. We're here on earth for that reason: to overcome our imperfections and one day become perfect, not in the eyes of the world, but perfect in the eyes of God.

For the longest time, I struggled with that word, "perfect." I felt it had to be immediate, and physically I was far from it and would need a miracle to look perfect. I misunderstood its meaning and came to understand that perfect can't be perfect without the imperfect, the weaknesses, the failures we experience, and the opposition.

Our earthly experience is to give us a chance to become perfect, "even as [our] Father which is in heaven is perfect" (Matthew 5:48). In mortality, we come to learn the necessity of opposition and the depth it adds to our mortal experience.

Dallin H. Oaks said, "All of us experience various kinds of opposition that test us. Some of these tests are temptations to sin. Some are mortal challenges apart from personal sin. Some are very great. Some are minor. Some are continuous, and some are mere episodes. None of us is exempt. Opposition permits us to grow toward what our Heavenly Father would have us become."[1]

The Lord said that He gave "unto men weakness that they may be humble . . . for if they humble themselves before me, and have faith in me, then will I make weak things become strong unto them" (Ether 12:27). Playing the piano bore witness to me of the Lord's promise to "make weak things become strong." My dad used to always say to me, "Fatai, if you want to succeed in life, you need to humble yourself." He was right.

Learning to play was really hard, and at times I just wanted to give up. But my desire to play the piano was greater than any frustration I could've felt. Instead, I sat at the piano keys trying to figure out how to play the music notes on sheet music. Praying for inspiration, the Lord showed me how, enabling me to see bits and pieces, until I was able to see the full picture of how my hands could play the piano, and hear the music my hands could create. It was a freeing experience and I was lifted with a new vision of what my life can be.

I am fortunate to have known about the gospel of Jesus Christ my whole life. I owe that to my parents. One evening, I was having a conversation with my dad about parenting and questioned some of his decisions that he made for me and my siblings when we were younger. His response left a deep impression on me as he said, "For me as a young father, I couldn't teach you everything. That's why I prayed for the Holy Ghost to teach you what I couldn't, and I lived to be worthy for that prayer to be answered." In that moment, I understood why I felt the Spirit often throughout my life. My dad faithfully prayed and lived for it, even like Alma did for his own son, that I might "be brought to the knowledge of the truth" (Mosiah 27:14). I am grateful to my father who made it a priority for us to feel the Holy Ghost work in our lives and remained faithful to see his prayer come to fruition.

As my knowledge and testimony grew in the gospel of Jesus Christ, I grew a dependence on the influence of the Holy Ghost. Music taught me more about the Spirit's voice. For the longest time, I couldn't understand what my dad meant when he'd say to me after every performance, "You didn't get it." I was always dumbfounded at his remark and would ask for him to explain what he meant. He'd usually respond with a, "You sing good, but you didn't get me." I would get frustrated, especially with his broken English, and think maybe he didn't know what he was talking about. Even though I was confused with my dad's words, I prayerfully studied it in my mind (see D&C 9:8) and practiced what I felt was the answer. It wasn't until I started feeling the Spirit of the Lord in my performances that I began to understand what my dad was trying to say. It was never about singing with my voice—it was all about singing with His.

I thought if I could sing as beautiful as Beyoncé and riff the heck out of my song, I'd sound amazing. But singing is more than just having a pretty voice. You can have the nicest vibrato and sing the most intricate runs, but your voice can still sound empty and can be past feeling. Singing has to come from a real place; it has to come from your heart. If it doesn't, your audience will know. They can feel when you're being fake. I have learned that singing is expressing your truth. It's being vulnerable, honest, and sincere. It's allowing others to experience your heart and soul regardless of its condition.

I found a piece of myself each time I sang about God. I came to know for myself of my worth and of my potential as I heard the voice of the Spirit testify to my spirit of eternal truths. I became a different person, born anew, as my soul began to understand what this voice, His voice, has been trying to tell me my whole life. Jesus is my Savior and Redeemer. He is the Christ. Because of him, my body will be perfected one day. I now know my body was prepared specifically for my spirit, a spirit at times I feel is too big for this body. But I trust in God's plan and know there is a reason. My hands were no mistake and were only meant to educate and enlighten. The Lord has blessed me greatly, and I have done my best to glorify Him by how I magnify His gifts He has given me.

I learned these truths "precept upon precept . . . line upon line; here a little, and there a little" (Isaiah 28:13). Learning to recognize the voice of the Spirit was like learning to recognize my baby's voice when I first became a mom. The first few weeks of her life, she slept most of the time. She would wake up every couple of hours crying to eat. I'd change her diaper, and she'd go right back to sleep. As she grew older, she was awake more and became more vocal. She mostly cried when she needed something. As time went on, I began to understand what her cries meant. Each cry had a different meaning. She had a cry for when she was tired or hungry. She had a cry for when she had a dirty diaper. As I spent more time with her, I got to know her voice more and what she needed.

On many occasions, we'd be visiting family or a friend and I would take my daughter to a quiet room to nap so as to keep her from all the noise that was going on. I'd leave her there to rest peacefully and rejoin everyone. Many times as we'd be busy socializing, I could hear faintly my daughter's voice amidst the noise in the room. I'd quickly run to check and see if she was in fact crying, and I would find her little voice crying in the room waiting to be rescued. I'd return with her and people would remark, "I didn't even hear her." I never really thought of how significant it was that I could recognize my own child's voice even amidst the noise. As I spent time with my daughter, it became easier for me to recognize her voice. It is the same with the Lord's voice.

When Jesus was speaking with his apostles, He taught, "And I will pray the Father, and He shall give you another Comforter, that He may abide with you forever; Even the Spirit of truth. . . . But the Comforter, which is the Holy Ghost, whom the Father will send in my name, he shall teach you all things, and bring all things to your remembrance, whatsoever I have said unto you" (John 14:16–17, 26). We can come to know the voice of the Spirit by spending quality time with the Lord. We can do that through constant scripture study, prayer and fasting, making and keeping covenants through sacred ordinances, service opportunities, and keeping His commandments.

Today, there are so many voices competing with the voice of the Spirit. We are taught in the scriptures that the voice of the Spirit is a still small voice, a voice of perfect mildness, a voice like unto a whisper, even piercing the very soul (see Helaman 5:30). This voice can easily be drowned out by the voices of the world if we let it. James E. Faust taught, "In your generation you will be barraged by multitudes of voices telling you how to live, how to gratify your passions, how to have it all. . . . Everyone will be under more scrutiny. There will be fewer places of refuge and serenity. You will be bombarded with evil and wickedness like no other generation."[2] It is crucial that we seek to be worthy to have the constant companionship of the Holy Ghost with us. Living the example of Christ will enable us to discern the voice of the Spirit from the voices of the world.

We each have the light of Christ within us that is the innate ability to know good from evil. "Wherefore, all things which are good cometh of God; and that which is evil cometh of the devil. . . . But behold, that which is of God inviteth and enticeth to do good continually; wherefore, every thing which inviteth and enticeth to do good, and to love God, and to serve him, is inspired of God. Wherefore, take heed, my beloved brethren, that ye do not judge that which is evil to be of God, or that which is good and of God to be of the devil" (Moroni 7:12–14).

One way I recognized the influence of the Spirit was in my feelings. The Apostle Paul described the spirit as feelings of "love, joy, peace, longsuffering, gentleness, goodness, faith" (Galatians 5:22). I have felt these feelings of the Spirit in times when I was seeking answers, and times when I felt like giving up. There was always a calm sense of assurance that all will be well, and so I sought to know more of Him because I wanted to be filled with the spirit of the Lord.

King Benjamin in the Book of Mormon posed a question to his people after they entered a covenant with God. He asked them, "For how knoweth the man whom he has not served, and who is a stranger unto him, and is far from the thoughts and intents of his heart?" (Mosiah 5:13). This question continually prompts me to examine my life, and I ask myself: How does service help me *know* the Lord? The lyrics to a favorite song come to mind:

My hands are the Lord's hands
Without me how can His work be done
I will reach where He will reach
Loving kindness in my touch
I'll be His healing hands to everyone.

My feet are the Lord's feet
Without me how can He walk with the poor

I will go where He would go
Blessing others as I do
For Him I'll walk where I've never walked before

Help me Lord. Let me give to my neighbor what You would
give if You were here.
Help me Lord. Let me live so my neighbor will know that
You are always near.

My mouth is the Lord's mouth
Without me how can His voice be heard
I will say what He would say
Speaking love and life each day
And everyone who's near will hear His word.[3]

The best way I was able to learn about God was by serving others. King Benjamin said, "When ye are in the service of your fellow beings ye are only in the service of your God," (Mosiah 2:17). I have come to know Him as I strived to follow Christ's example in how I live my life. There were times where I didn't fully understand the reason behind some of the things the Lord asked of me, but in listening to that still small voice, I felt closest to the Lord when I obediently followed those promptings, and in return, was greatly blessed for it.

Two years after I had my second child, I was pregnant with our third. I was excited to enter my second trimester because I was experiencing severe morning sickness throughout the first trimester. One morning, I had woken up feeling *empty* in my belly. A quick thought came to my mind, *Oh, no. Something's wrong with the baby.* But I brushed that thought aside and thought maybe I was hungry.

A few weeks later, I had my doctor's appointment. As my doctor did a routine check, searching for the baby's heartbeat, I began to worry as she took longer than usual to find it. Moving her hand around, she reassured me that maybe the baby was in a position that made it difficult for her to catch the heartbeat. She needed to check with the ultrasound machine. She left to grab the machine, and I could not help but think about that morning I woke up feeling empty inside my belly. She wheeled in a small ultrasound machine and looked hopeful that she would find something. As she began to probe around my belly, we could see the baby's silhouette laying perfectly still. My fear was confirmed, and we saw the baby's heart had indeed stopped beating.

As I reflect back to that morning I had awoken feeling *empty*, I knew then that emptiness I felt was indeed the absence of the precious spirit of that child. I was deeply impressed at the power of that baby's spirit. For the spirit to leave a distinct absence, I was in awe of this baby's potential and was reminded of Peter's words of great and precious promises that are given us as "partakers of the divine nature" (2 Peter 1:4). Each one of us come to this world with the potential to live up to our birthright as "heirs of God; and joint-heirs with Christ" (Romans 8:16–17).

In "The Family: A Proclamation to the World," it states that "all human beings—male and female—are created in the image of God. Each is a beloved spirit son or daughter of heavenly parents, and, as such, each has a divine nature and destiny."[4] Imagine the great things you can accomplish if you truly realized your divine potential. You would know with a surety of who you are as a child of God. You would desire to serve those in need. You would stay focused on meaningful goals, seek for higher learning, utilize your gifts and talents to bless others, and continue to develop the divine potential within you.

As you remember Him, you remember who you are. You'll need to remember Him especially when you feel like you're failing at life. This life was meant to test our ability to remember

Him or not. I've always felt like our life on earth is one big lesson plan God created for each of us. Because we each have unique spirits, each lesson plan is tailor-made to each one of us. He made it that way because we all learn differently, and we all come to earth in need of acquiring skills, knowledge, and experience that shall be for our good (see D&C 122:7).

Life's lessons are meant to refine us to our ultimate self that God knows us to be. These lessons continue to teach us, mold us, refine us until we have mastered each lesson and have taken one step closer to becoming and fully realizing our God-given potential. But I've learned to not get comfortable for there is always another lesson unfolding, preparing itself to challenge you. Thomas S. Monson said,

> We learn and grow and become stronger as we face and survive the trials through which we must pass. We know that there are times when we will experience heartbreaking sorrow, when we will grieve, and when we may be tested to our limits. However, such difficulties allow us to change for the better, to rebuild our lives in the way our Heavenly Father teaches us, and to become something different from what we were— better than we were, more understanding than we were, more empathetic than we were, with stronger testimonies than we had before.
>
> This should be our purpose—to persevere and endure, yes, but also to become more spiritually refined as we make our way through sunshine and sorrow. Were it not for challenges to overcome and problems to solve, we would remain much as we are, with little or no progress toward our goal of eternal life.[5]

Growing up, I never imagined myself to be a mother. It was always an afterthought. Honestly, I was not good with kids. Whenever my mom "volun-told" me to babysit, I'd make my sisters help. Babies did not like me. I didn't mean to make them cry, but they did not like my facial expressions when I'd play peek-a-boo. They must've sensed my fear because I avoided holding babies in fear that I might hold them incorrectly and even break them with my hands. When I became a mom, my insecurities resurfaced, and I had no choice but to revisit them. I knew how I had triumphed these insecurities, but I had to brace myself for new lessons that would test my faith, my intuition, and my worth as a woman and as a daughter of God.

I gave birth to four beautiful children: two girls and two boys. With every child I had, I thought it impossible for my heart to love another child. But I am amazed at the heart and its capacity to love. It knows no bounds and is infinite. It's a tender mercy for me to get a glimpse of the amount of love God has for each of us. You'd think it's crazy that God can love and care for us all when there's so many of us; but he does. He truly does love and care for each one of us. He is aware of you and hopes you will turn to Him for help as any good parent hopes for their child.

Becoming a mom redefined what love meant. I never knew that kind of love could be born out of physical pain and suffering. The only word I can describe my first time going through the whole labor and delivery process for me was traumatic. I was traumatized and was ill-prepared for the whole experience. I had mentally prepared myself for the worst. When I was experiencing excruciating bone-breaking pain, I told myself that things could be worse than this and continued to endure. My plan was to have my baby natural, having no anesthesia. When my contractions slowed down, I was given *pitocin*, a medicine used to basically force your body to have the baby. Determined to follow my plan, I declined having anesthesia and suffered the most physical pain I ever felt in my life.

Even with this traumatic experience of giving birth to my baby girl, the moment I heard her cry, I was overwhelmed with love that I bawled my eyes out. It's true when they say that even after all the pain you experience from labor and the delivery that you forget the pain the moment you see your baby or hear their first cry. But you forget the pain for just a moment. I was quickly brought back to reality as they began my recovery process. In need of stitches, I felt even more pain, and I might dare say it was more painful than the laboring and birthing process. Keep in mind, I still didn't use any form of anesthesia. I can't believe I listened to my mom to have my baby naturally.

My recovery in the hospital was painful. They gave me pain medication which numbed the pain my body felt, but what I really needed was medication for my mind. My mind kept the pain alive, and I was still in shock with what my body had just experienced. Having the support of my husband and my mom during those first few weeks helped tremendously with my recovery.

Becoming a mom, I had so many questions. I felt so many fears. I doubted in my capabilities as a new mother and felt lost. I watched my mom care for my daughter the first few weeks of her life. That was a tender mercy as I was struggling to recover from giving birth. The day my mom left, I remember looking at my daughter's face and beginning to cry. I forgot everything and was unsure I could be a mom. My mom wasn't here to show me how to care for my baby. Nursing was still a struggle, and I was still getting used to the feeding schedule. Sleep deprivation affected my mood swings. My poor husband had to deal with a cranky wife 24/7. My body no longer looked the same, and I felt like I had lost a part of myself.

With all the struggles I was experiencing those first few weeks, it did get better. I was feeling more comfortable taking care of my daughter. Nursing improved. I was beginning to figure out her schedule. I started to understand what her cries meant which was a big deal. I felt sure of myself and my momma skills. As my daughter grew, I was unaware of the changes that were happening within me.

I began noticing behavioral changes within me. I felt enormous pressure to do things right, and for any new mom knows, those first few months is all a guessing game. That's all you're doing, guessing what your baby needs and trying to understand what their cries mean. I would just break down and cry out of nowhere and I sometimes couldn't understand why. I started noticing how empty I felt as I would stare at my baby. I knew I should be feeling joy and love for her, but I felt nothing. I scared myself many times of "what if" thoughts of my baby dying. With all of these new feelings I was experiencing, I was second guessing myself and began to question my worth.

When I went to my six-week check-up with my doctor, she noticed a change in my behavior and asked how I was doing. I broke down crying. I told her, "I don't know why I feel so sad when I know I should be happy to have my baby."

She responded, "You have the baby blues, Leslie." That was the first time I ever heard that term. The baby blues. She continued to tell me about postpartum depression and how it's common for mothers to experience these symptoms after having a baby. Depression? I was depressed? I was in shock that I was experiencing this form of depression.

I experienced depression when I was a teen and vowed not to ever go back to that dark place. But I was in shock that I experienced depression again at what was supposed to be a joyful time in my life. My doctor offered to prescribe some medication to help, and I accepted. As I took the medication the first couple days, I did see an improvement in my mood swings, but inside, my spirit felt numb. I didn't like that feeling. I stopped taking the medication. If I was going to get better, I needed to start with my spirit. So I began my journey to recovery from depression once again.

I began to rely heavily on the Lord. I knew if I were to be healed from this depression, I needed to feel his Spirit with me again, to awaken my soul (see 2 Nephi 4:28). I started searching the scriptures more. I prayed like I never did before. I made an extra effort to be at church every Sunday just to partake the sacrament. I sought to secure blessings I was in desperate need of through obedience to God's commandments and through my faithfulness in service.

I received priesthood blessings from my husband when I really needed it most. I have always felt safe and secure when he worthily exercised his priesthood duty to bless me and our family. I reached out to trusted friends and family I knew could be a support. Most of the time, I just needed someone to talk to. I have been blessed with some of the best visiting teachers. Those sisters who visited me faithfully will never fully understand what those visits meant to me. Their testimonies were exactly what I needed to remind me of my own testimony. Now, I don't mean to say that this is the proven way to curing depression. For some, you'll need professional help and might need the assistance of medication. But I found what worked best for me.

After I had baby number four, I quickly recognized I was experiencing symptoms of postpartum depression again. I prayerfully began the process to healing again. Having to experience depression several times throughout my life, I began to ask the Lord, "What have I not learned yet?" This time around I began to understand the importance to "live in thanksgiving daily, for the many mercies and blessings" (Alma 34:38) that the Lord gives us.

Elder Dieter F. Uchtdorf profoundly stated, "We sometimes think that being grateful is what we do after our problems are solved, but how terribly short-sighted that is. How much of life do we miss by waiting to see the rainbow before thanking God that there is rain? Being grateful in times of distress does not mean that we are pleased with our circumstances. It does mean that through the eyes of faith we look beyond our present-day challenges. This is not a gratitude of the lips but of the soul. It is a gratitude that heals the heart and expands the mind."[6] Seeking out the good amidst the trial lightens the load our hearts carry. We begin to hope that deliverance is nigh and in the process learn to enjoy the journey. I don't know if I'll experience depression again, but I do know that I can rely on the Lord to help me through whatever trial I face.

As we realize who we are as a child of God, we understand our self-worth by understanding who God is, and in so doing, we emulate Him in our being. Feeling God's love has been the motivation behind every decision I make. It changed me into who I am today, and it keeps me going knowing, inevitably, I will fall over and over again. But I cannot forget His love, His mercy, and His grace that saves me each time I do.

Elder Ronald A. Rasband said, "Never forget, question, or ignore personal, sacred spiritual experiences. The adversary's design is to distract us from spiritual witnesses, while the Lord's desire is to enlighten and engage us in His work. . . . In the midst of life's greatest storms, do not forget your divine heritage as a son or daughter of God or your eternal destiny to one day return to live with Him, which will surpass anything the world has to offer."[7]

Being born with only five fingers, what I thought would be a trial became my biggest blessing in disguise. I wasted so much time and energy focusing on what I lacked that I failed to recognize the blessings that I did have. I have learned important life lessons of acceptance, faith, hope, charity, and gratitude. I know I would not be the person that I am today if it weren't for my struggles as I had to trust in the Lord's ways with all my heart (see Proverbs 3:5–6). I have come to know with a surety that "I can do all things through Christ which strengtheneth me" (Philippians 4:13). And as I come unto Christ and feel His love, I can hear my heart song and it is beautiful: What I have is enough.

NOTES

1. Dallin H. Oaks, "Opposition in All Things," *Ensign*, May 2016.
2. James E. Faust, "The Voice of the Spirit" (Brigham Young University devotional, September 5, 1993), speeches.byu.edu.
3. "My Hands," Bright Cloud Music, 1989, lyrics by Carol Lynn Pearson, music by Lex de Azevedo.
4. "The Family: A Proclamation to the World," *Ensign,* November 2010, 129.
5. Thomas S. Monson, "I Will Not Fail Thee, nor Forsake Thee," *Ensign*, November 2013.
6. Dieter F. Uchtdorf, "Grateful in Any Circumstances," *Ensign*, May 2014.
7. Ronald A. Rasband, "Lest Thou Forget," *Ensign*, November 2016.

About the Author

Leslie Fatai was born and raised in Utah. She was born with a limb deficiency in her hands having only five fingers. Many are surprised to learn that she can play the piano and are fascinated to watch her play it. She is married to a supportive husband and is a mother to four young children. Currently, she's working to make all her songs available on sheet music and plans to continue writing new material. You can learn more about Leslie on her website at www.lesliefatai.com.

Scan to visit

www.lesliefatai.com